12 More Stupid Things That Mess Up Recovery

12 More Stupid Things That Mess Up Recovery

Navigating Common Pitfalls on Your Sobriety Journey

ALLEN BERGER, Ph.D.

Hazelden Publishing
Center City, Minnesota 55012
hazelden.org/bookstore

ISBN: 978-1-61649-654-8; ebook 978-1-61649-655-5
Library of Congress Cataloging-in-Publication Data is on file at the Library of Congress.

Editor's notes
The names, details, and circumstances have been changed to protect the privacy of those mentioned in this publication. See the author's note on page 10.

This publication is not intended as a substitute for the advice of health care professionals.

Alcoholics Anonymous, AA, and the Big Book are registered trademarks of Alcoholics Anonymous World Services, Inc.

This book was reissued in 2023 with a new cover and minor editing updates.

27 26 25 24 23   1 2 3 4 5 6

Developmental editor: Sid Farrar
Production editor: Mindy Keskinen
Cover design: Nick Caruso Design
Cover illustration: Gerard DuBois
Interior design and typesetting: Jennifer Dolezal and
David Farr, *ImageSmythe*

Dedication

To Madelynn Rose Berger, born on March 15, 2013, whose conception and journey into this world taught me a great lesson, as readers will see in this book.

I love you, Maddy—forever!

Contents

Foreword by Fred H.

I first met Allen Berger in Vermont at a fall conference of New England doctors in recovery. Each of us had been invited to present on the theme of emotional sobriety. Although our approaches were very different, they both centered on Bill W.'s 1958 *Grapevine* article "The Next Frontier—Emotional Sobriety." This seminal document describes what we do in recovery that contributes to our "defective relations with other human beings" and, as importantly, why we do it.

That weekend, as students of AA history, Allen and I quickly came to appreciate our deep interest, personally and professionally, in Bill W.'s uncanny grasp of the human condition. A year and a half later, I was with him on a larger panel discussing his "Unpacking Bill Wilson's 1956 Letter on Emotional Sobriety" at the annual conference of International Doctors in Alcoholics Anonymous. I feel blessed to have worked with someone who brings to his writing such a unique combination of professionalism, knowledge of Twelve Step principles, and the ability to articulate the practical lessons he's learned as teacher, therapist, sponsor, and human being. Which is why I am especially delighted to have the opportunity to write the foreword to Allen's newest addition to his growing list of important contributions to the body of recovery literature.

As with his previous works, this book somehow makes the problem of addiction less baffling and its Twelve Step solution less mysterious. The authenticity of these "twelve more stupid things" is verified as soon as you read them. For me, the cautionary lessons from my own story—such as magical thinking, private logic, reacting to the present as though it's the past, spiritual pride, and self-righteousness—jumped off each page. And I was reminded in more than one instance of the work I have in front of me today. This is good stuff for both newcomers and old-timers—though, aren't we all really newcomers each day?

One of the warnings in the Big Book about Step Ten is how easy it is to "let up on the spiritual program of action and rest on our laurels." This human tendency is triggered by the peace of mind and serenity that our practice of the Steps promises and delivers. The memory of the powerlessness and unmanageability that Step One dramatically brought to our attention may have begun to fade over the horizon. Allen's book gives us a comprehensive exposure to the unmanageability of a more "living" or "real-time" Step One. When we begin to realize the various ways that we still awaken that unmanageability—and then we begin to apply Twelve Step principles and practices to restore our physical and emotional sobriety—we find touchstones for continued growth throughout each day. That we continue to live out the unmanageability of Step One, even in long-term recovery, is a manifestation of our disease. There'll always be a vestige of powerlessness in the "slowest part of us to get well," the part of us where our "twelve more stupid things" have their being. And guess what? Addiction is a chronic illness—there'll always be some part of us getting well.

When you read this book, you won't wind up feeling twelve ways more stupid. Its gift will be the realization that your naiveté and imperfections are simply the day-to-day problems *that need your attention,* so that, one day at a time, you won't have to revisit the problem *that got your attention* in the first place.

Fred Holmquist
Director of the Lodge Program at the Dan Anderson Renewal Center
Hazelden Betty Ford Foundation

Acknowledgments

An interesting thing happened as I was beginning to write this follow-up to my first book for Hazelden Publishing, *12 Stupid Things That Mess Up Recovery.* I was struggling to find a rhythm. I'd get started in a certain direction and then hit an impasse. Sid Farrar, my editor at Hazelden, sensed that I was having trouble and asked me if I needed help. "Yes," I responded, feeling both relieved and embarrassed. You see, even after all this time, it's hard for me to ask for what I need and let someone else see that I need help.

Sid was able to arrange for writer-editor Vince Hyman to help me develop the early drafts of this book, and I was immediately heartened. Vince had worked with me on *12 Smart Things to Do When the Booze and Drugs Are Gone.* He gets my work; he understands how I think and the message I am trying to convey. This creates a powerful synergy between the two of us, which brings the best out in me. Without the unwavering support I received from both Sid and Vince, this book wouldn't have become a reality, and I thank them for their faith in my work.

I also want to acknowledge the contributions from DocDawn and Dr. Harry. They are paving the way for the next generation of medical doctors to be more informed about recovery. Herb Kaighan and Tom McCall, my sponsor, also made several significant contributions to this book, and I'm grateful for their love and support.

Introduction

The Recovery Odyssey

The recovery odyssey is immensely rewarding—but it can also be difficult at times. You'll have moments when you feel serene and grounded, but there will also be times when you'll feel lost, confused, or overwhelmed. On this adventure you will encounter many twists and turns, and some rough and challenging terrain. There will even be times of so much discomfort, struggle, and frustration that you'll feel like giving up and wonder if the journey is worth it. But if you stay the course, you'll also be lifted to great heights and witness some breathtaking vistas.

It's quite possible that the recovery trek will feel like one of the most difficult journeys of your life. But I can promise you this much: if you can stay the course, it's a journey that is worth taking and will change you forever in ways you cannot yet imagine.

Working a "fearless and thorough" recovery program will deepen your understanding of yourself and your important relationships. You will realize your true potential and see life from a new perspective. On this trek you'll discover that what we *think* is the problem is seldom the real problem—that life "is what it is," and that how we cope with the challenges of life is what makes them either a problem or a learning experience.

If you work an honest and rigorous Twelve Step program, the Big Book of *Alcoholics Anonymous* promises that you will experience moments when you are truly amazed and filled with wonder and pure joy. You will know happiness, serenity, and peace of mind. Of course you will also know disappointment, sadness, and grief—but it's in facing these difficult feelings and working through them that you will recover your lost true self, discover new possibilities, and fully engage with life. You will come to recognize some of your habitual and outdated ways of thinking and reacting, and you'll replace them with healthier options. You will live your life with greater self-awareness and an expanded consciousness. The nature of true self-esteem and spirituality will be revealed. You will discover parts of yourself that you'd lost touch with. As a result, you'll reduce the destructive influences of your false self and reinstate the constructive forces of your true self.

But recovery will also ruin a number of your favorite habitual ideas and behaviors. Most important, you will never be able to look at drinking or using the way you did before you started the journey. It will also become harder for you to compromise your integrity when faced with moral decisions. You will find it difficult to remain passive, to tolerate being a victim, and to wallow in self-pity when faced with the burdens of life.

I like to think of recovery as a *journey of discovery* that opens up new possibilities for well-being. But only if you're willing to face this paradox: you must experience discomfort in order to find the comfort that a life of recovery brings.

Recovery is like taking an arduous hike. The Kalalau Trail on the island of Kauai, Hawaii, which is listed among the top ten most difficult hikes in America, makes for a great analogy. This eleven-mile adventure takes you along the dramatic and lush Na Pali Coast. If you saw the opening scenes of the first *Jurassic Park* movie, you'll remember the breathtaking aerial shots of the tropical jungle and waterfall on this beautiful island.

When you start any hike, finding the right trailhead is the first challenge. Often the signage is incomplete or confusing. Similarly, as you begin your recovery, the signposts and trailheads might bewilder you, marked by various ads and advice for recovery "consumers." Just like choosing a trailhead for exploring Kauai, you have to discover the path that works best for you in meeting your particular needs and desires.

For example, if you choose the Kalalau trailhead, you'll soon realize that you're in for one heck of a trek. The trail is narrow and uneven, which in certain places makes it hard to keep your balance because you can't find solid footing. On other stretches you'll find yourself cruising along and enjoying the magnificent views of the coastline. Some people who have taken this hike have fallen off the path to their death. Many have turned back because it was just too difficult or unnerving. It's the same with recovery. We have lost many of our recovery brothers and sisters who have fallen off the path and died from a relapse or a drug-related accident. Others have just dropped out of the scene and are nowhere to be found. But many also find the right tools and guides—the same things you need to navigate a treacherous trail—to successfully face the challenges of the recovery journey and enjoy the rewards of its magnificent views.

The Kalalau Trail becomes even more dangerous when it rains. The rain turns the path into a greasy slip-n-slide that is terrifying when you're edging along a 300-foot cliff that spills straight down onto the rocky surf. One misstep could cause you to fall to your death. There are parallels here to the dangers of the recent opioid painkiller and heroin epidemic, where death through an overdose or a drug-related accident has become all too common.

The Kalalau Trail can also be deceptive. You may be sailing along and everything seems peachy, and then just around the bend you run into a stretch of trail that seems impassable. Similarly, in recovery, everything can seem to be going well with our program and there'll be an unexpected crisis that can throw us for a loop. But as with going on an arduous hike, the more we can predict, understand, and prepare for the ups and downs that lie ahead, the better we can cope with these challenges when we face them.

In psychology we refer to this as *anticipatory coping*. Anticipating a problem helps us mobilize the resources within and outside of ourselves to handle it better.

Anticipating what might come your way in recovery is the rationale behind this book, as it was for its predecessor, *12 Stupid Things That Mess Up Recovery*. I want to make you aware of some of the pitfalls that you might encounter on your recovery trek and what you can do to prevent them—or cope with them when they happen.

Recovery becomes difficult, if not downright impossible, when we try to make this trek alone. If we take a tough hike with someone who already knows the trail, we'll be in a better position when we hit a hard stretch or we pause at a fork and wonder which way to go. The same is true for the recovery journey. I believe that we all need a guide—what I call an *enlightened witness*—involved in our recovery. This role can be fulfilled by anyone we trust—a program sponsor, a wise therapist, a spiritual director, or a trusted alcohol and drug counselor.

I've had the same sponsor since 1971. Tom has been there for me whenever I've needed him. He showed faith in me when I had very little faith in myself. When I floundered, he supported me emotionally until I could stand on my own two feet and provide myself with the support I needed. He helped me navigate some difficult terrain when I sabotaged my recovery by creating a personal crisis. During those dark times, which were filled with anxiety and dread, he helped me decide on the best direction to reclaim my personal integrity. With Tom's unwavering support and love, I have been enjoying a clean and sober life since 1971.

Even though a book like this can't do everything an enlightened witness can, supporting you in every step you take in recovery, it can provide you with some guidelines and advice based on how others have navigated their trek.

In my first book I discussed twelve common pitfalls you might encounter in the first couple of years in recovery. Although readers have told me that those issues are relevant beyond that time frame, I decided that another book—this one—was warranted to address issues that occur in both early recovery and beyond.

The "twelve more stupid things" discussed here are pitfalls that can cause significant setbacks and prevent you from receiving all the benefits of this amazing journey. At worst, they can send you back into the nightmare of active addiction.

No one among us has been able to completely avoid falling off the path or getting lost during our trek. We are humans and therefore will make mistakes and poor decisions. The important thing is that we pick ourselves back up when we have fallen, find our way back when we are lost, and get on with the business of learning from our mistakes. This is the essence of real long-term recovery. It's about learning, and learning is about discovering new possibilities.

You'll learn about these twelve more pitfalls in the following twelve chapters. Let's preview them here first.

1. *Waiting for your fairy godmother.* While there are many paths to getting and staying sober, it's your responsibility, and no one else's, to find the path that's best for you.
2. *Conning yourself by labeling passivity as "acceptance and surrender."* Passivity means letting things happen without claiming our role in events. Real acceptance and surrender involve actively taking responsibility for the things we can change and accepting the things we cannot.
3. *Confusing meeting attendance with working a program.* We call it working a program because it takes effort! Simply sitting at a meeting is too passive. Confronting yourself, striving to have the best possible attitude, finding the right help or the right sponsor, and actively practicing the Steps is what matters.
4. *Failing to understand and develop a healthy relationship with your addict or alcoholic self.* Addiction has changed us in many ways, both physically and mentally. As our illness progressed, we developed an addict or alcoholic self that joined the rest of the selves that populate us. Over time, that self took complete control of our personality. Even now, in recovery, it's still with us. And if we ignore or underestimate that addict or alcoholic self, we're at a high risk for relapse. Our best chance in recovery is to get to know that self and to learn how to coordinate the rest of our selves with it.
5. *Discounting the creeping thoughts that you can drink or use again.* The addict self is tenacious: it looks for any chance to justify picking up a drink or using again. These creeping thoughts are bound to happen. Being ashamed of

them, or feeling like we need to keep them a secret, will sabotage our recovery. We need to share these thoughts with someone we trust and try to understand what they mean or what they're telling us.

6. *Listening to others when you need to listen to your own best self.* See Stupid Thing 1—the fairy godmother syndrome. No one is right all the time, and working the Steps or any other program does not call for us to check our brains at the door—quite the opposite! Sponsors and others, even professionals, may give advice that contradicts program principles or our own intuition.
7. *Using prescribed mind-altering drugs when other remedies are available.* Mind-altering drugs such as medical marijuana or opioids may be needed for certain conditions, but recovery requires that we use other remedies when we can. These drugs can endanger our sobriety, so we should be sure to find medical doctors who understand our disease, prescribe these drugs only when no other treatments work, and monitor us closely.
8. *Shaming yourself (or others) for relapse.* Relapse is a common characteristic of the chronic disease of addiction. When we hide a relapse because of shame or fear of what others think—or on the other hand, when we discredit someone else who has relapsed—we set up conditions that perpetuate addiction. Seeking help for relapse is to be praised, not shamed.
9. *Clinging to toxic attitudes that sabotage recovery.* We need to strive to replace toxic attitudes and beliefs with ones

that will add to who we are, that are nourishing and nurturing to our recovery.

10. *Donning a white robe and halo when you need to be digging in the muck.* The spirituality to be discovered and uncovered through working the Twelve Steps offers a remarkable way of life. But believing that you don't need to deal with personal issues because you have found an all-encompassing "spiritual solution" to your problems—a spiritual bypass—is simply a way to avoid the, at times, painful, difficult, and muddy work of self-discovery and healing.
11. *Insisting that reality conform to your expectations.* Life presents us with its own terms, and our job is to learn to live with them. Failure to manage our expectations is a setup for unhappiness and relapse.
12. *Working only the first eleven Steps and not integrating service work into your recovery.* Service work—helping others through loving action—takes time and effort, and it is a key to long-term sobriety, emotional health, and self-actualization.

You will see that four important and interrelated themes emerge from these twelve pitfalls: passivity, multiple selves, toxic attitudes, and expectations.

Passivity is destructive to recovery, and it's a common problem among people at all stages of recovery. The solution to passivity is not simply to act but rather to mobilize yourself to become responsive and responsible. You'll read about passivity in several of the twelve chapters that follow—notably "Waiting for Your Fairy Godmother," "Conning Yourself by Labeling Passivity as 'Acceptance and Surrender,'" "Confusing Meeting Attendance with Working a

Program," and "Listening to Others When You Need to Listen to Your Own Best Self."

I believe that the Twelve Steps offer us a way to come to grips with who we truly are—and that failing to do so means we miss the great benefit of recovery and raise our risk of relapse. As we come to grips with ourselves, we get to know the *multiple selves* within us. In this book, several of the twelve stupid things refer to our various selves and what we can learn from them—including, believe it or not, the importance of accepting and learning from our alcoholic or addict self. In fact, you'll learn that your emotional well-being depends on coordinating all that you are. A related theme is the importance of rediscovering and trusting our inner voice—the voice that knows what is truly right for us. This is a voice, a self, that we learned to ignore as we followed the path of addiction, but one we must rediscover as we gain a sense of a healthy self in recovery. You'll find the theme *multiple selves* in "Failing to Understand and Develop a Healthy Relationship with Your Addict or Alcoholic Self," "Discounting the Creeping Thoughts That You Can Drink or Use Again," and "Listening to Others When You Need to Listen to Your Own Best Self."

Another important theme in this book is the effect of *toxic attitudes* on our recovery. By focusing our awareness on the quality of our thoughts or beliefs, we can identify them as either nurturing to our recovery or toxic to it. You'll find this theme in "Listening to Others When You Need to Listen to Your Own Best Self," "Shaming Yourself (or Others) for Relapse," "Clinging to Toxic Attitudes That Sabotage Recovery," and "Donning a White Robe and Halo When You Need to Be Digging in the Muck."

Expectations are a component of toxic attitudes, since most toxic attitudes include some sort of "should" that governs us. But one overarching expectation rules them all, so much so that it's the final theme in the book. You'll see that our expectations about how life should be can cause problems for us. You'll find this theme in "Insisting That Reality Conform to Your Expectations."

Throughout this book, you'll see real-life examples through my clients' stories (I've changed their names and other identifying details to protect their anonymity). I'll also tell you some stories from my own recovery journey.

Each chapter also includes a series of questions that you can use to further explore how these issues relate to your recovery. Please keep a pen and paper, or your laptop, close by and interact with these questions. They'll help you identify issues that may sabotage your recovery.

Thank you for allowing me to join you on your journey. Let's trudge this road of recovery and remove these barriers to our Happy Destiny together.

Stupid Thing 1

Waiting for Your Fairy Godmother

While there are many paths to getting and staying sober,
it's your responsibility, and no one else's,
to find the path that's best for you.

When you begin recovery, you embark on a journey that will change your life in unimaginable ways. It's normal to ask, "What path is best for me to get sober and stay sober, and how will I find it?" Once you've been in recovery for a while, you begin to ask something like, "Is the path I've been on the best one for me?"

These are good questions. But we often expect that there is a simple, single answer. We also hope for a guru or fairy godmother of some sort—someone who will magically pick us up and put us on the right path. But that's unrealistic, as you will learn in this chapter. In fact, that very expectation is pretty much a repetition of what we were doing when we were drinking or using—trying to find a magical, single answer for our screwed-up life. It didn't work then, and it won't work any better now. All we're doing is repeating a failed behavior. And that's the first thing to know about addiction: people with addiction have trouble learning from experience.

They repeat the same behaviors that got them into trouble in the first place. Where did this magical expectation come from? Why do we persist in believing there is only one right path? Why do we rigidly stick to a path, even when experience shows us that it leads nowhere?

In this chapter, I hope to help you answer these questions. But let's start with some important information about who we are as alcoholics and addicts.

Failing to Learn from Our Experience

In the psychological literature about active alcoholics and addicts, this point is clear: we don't learn from our experience. And that also creates a problem when it comes to identifying the best path for us to take in our recovery. You see, we need to use our experience to become aware of if what we're doing is, in fact, helpful—if it is right for us. Why do we fail to learn? Learning occurs when we process the feedback we get from a behavior and use it to enhance our awareness. A child learns not to touch a hot stove by touching it and getting burned. A child eats ice cream and wants more because it is pleasurable. If she then eats too much and gets sick, she may learn when to stop the next time. The pain or pleasure that the child experiences tells the child what's in her best interest.

We alcoholics and addicts have lost this simplicity in our lives. How many times have you been hurt as a result of drinking or using? Probably too many, but despite the pain and suffering it has caused you or your loved ones, you returned to drinking or using again. Repeatedly ignoring the messages and warnings of our inner voice desensitizes us to the role experience plays in learning.

In AA meetings we hear the definition of insanity as "doing the same thing and expecting different results." Well, I believe the problem is much worse than that—we do the same thing and expect *better* results. Better? Are you kidding me? We are sincerely deluded. Clearly we are not learning from our experience. So the question becomes, What is blocking us from seeing the obvious and admitting our fatal condition?

We fool ourselves by dulling our awareness. This desensitization begins early in life. At a young age, most of us dedicated ourselves to trying to be someone we thought we *should* be rather than staying true to who we were. We wanted to please our parents, our teachers, or siblings, our friends—and that often meant ignoring who *we* were and what pleased *us*. Even though that hurt us in countless ways, we often continued to choose the rewards of others' approval over finding out who we were and what we wanted. We cut ourselves off, numbed ourselves with alcohol and other drugs, and avoided becoming aware of the truth about ourselves, including the impact of our drinking and using. And in recovery, many of us persist in this behavior. By continuing to look for magical answers outside of ourselves, we avoid becoming aware of what really works for us, and what doesn't.

And we become passive, which is deadly to recovery. We stay locked in a childish belief that there is one solution to our problems, that one person or path holds all the answers. Let's dig into what that means, and how passivity can sabotage recovery.

The Toxic Effects of Passivity on Recovery

Passivity makes it less likely that we will discover our path to full, mature recovery. Why? Because when we are passive, we marginalize the role of our true self in determining our path. We leave ourselves out of the process of our own recovery! *Passivity separates us from being an active, determining force in our own lives.* Regardless of the path we choose, we'll need to be an active part of the process. In the words of recovery author and counselor Earnie Larsen, "If nothing changes, nothing changes." I would put it this way: if we don't change our passive attitude toward ourselves and our problems, then nothing will change.

Passivity interferes with taking the necessary steps that will help us find the best path for our recovery. Passivity leads us to wait for something to happen rather than mobilizing to make something happen. *Our full personal participation in finding the optimal path to recovery is essential to our success.* Passivity will undermine our attempt to create a better life.

Passivity almost undermined my own early recovery back in 1971. I unconsciously hoped that someone would come along and tell me what was best for me. That's the fairy godmother syndrome. I wanted someone to figure out what I needed to do and show me the easiest way to get sober and stay sober. What an order! I wanted to be saved, to be rescued from my self-destructive behavior and from my addiction, but I wanted to be a passive participant in the process. Quite a paradox.

If you'd met me back then, you wouldn't have guessed that I was so passive. I hid it well. I was great at asserting myself in the public areas of my life, but not when it came to taking care of myself or protecting myself. I had quickly climbed the ranks in the Marine Corps, becoming a corporal in less than two years. I ended up as section chief on a base piece in an artillery unit, overseeing a gun crew that ensured the artillery battery was accurately targeted. It was an important role; I had to be direct and give orders ensuring that every crew member was carrying his weight. That I could do. But when it came to talking about something I personally needed, I fell mute.

Over the years I've come to understand that my passivity in early recovery was in part due to the fact that I wanted my future to reverse the experiences of my past. I hoped that something would happen in the future to compensate for the painful times in my early life, rather than seeing the future as one I created by seeking to know and express my true desires. This passive attitude undermined my ability to act on my own behalf. In fact, losing my father at the critical age of twelve was partly responsible for this passivity. I was devastated when he died. You see, I loved my dad deeply and idealized him—he was everything to me: so funny, knowledgeable, strong, loving, and capable. My sense of worship and dependency on him was probably appropriate for that age, so when he passed away he left a big hole in my life. I missed his guidance and support through the tough years of adolescence when I was trying to figure out my own identity. I imagine that if he'd been present during my teens, he would have helped me learn how to stand on my own two feet—though I will never know. But I do know this: I needed the support of a man to become a man.

On December 26, 1963, I was told that my father had passed away the night before in the hospital. I fell into a deep, inconsolable grief. I was hurt, bitter, and angry, but I didn't let anyone see it. My mother and my father's dad, my grandpa, were devastated. Their pain and loss seemed to occupy all the emotional space in our family. I didn't believe there was any room for my feelings. I suffered alone, never expressing my feelings, never once asking for comfort. I didn't want to add to their burdens, so I shut down. I felt alone, and a deep sense of desperation overcame me.

I had lost my father and felt abandoned by my mother and grandfather. But another part of me emerged that day that I unconsciously believed would ensure my future well-being. I developed an unconscious claim that my future life should conform to my needs, make up for my loss, supply me with love and comfort, and provide me with a father who would ensure my full initiation into manhood. I felt like God or someone owed me this much, since my father was so unfairly taken from my life and since no one was there for me when I needed comfort and support.

So, after floundering through my high-school years, I signed up for a three-year commitment with the Marines at age seventeen, hoping it would help me become a man. I wanted something or someone to help me feel better about myself, because my self-esteem was in the toilet. I had no concept of the various forces that were driving my life at that time—I didn't know what I didn't know.

I attended boot camp at the San Diego Marine Corps Recruit Depot for a grueling sixteen weeks, learning close-quarter drill, hand-to-hand combat, physical fitness, rifle care, and marksmanship, and being indoctrinated with the thinking and behavior that make a Marine. It was one of the hardest challenges I've ever faced. So you'd think that at the graduation ceremony, when I was officially awarded the title of US Marine and pinned with the globe and anchor initiating me into the ranks of manhood, I would have felt proud of myself. In fact, I felt the opposite: I felt like a phony. I thought that they'd made a mistake letting my scrawny little ass graduate and enter the ranks of the few and the proud. This should have been my first tip that my search for a fairy godmother wasn't going to turn out as I hoped it would, but I was too young to understand the lesson. Graduation from boot camp clearly hadn't made up for my losses or healed the wounds to my self-esteem. Today I see that it did many other beneficial things for me, but it couldn't make me whole. I realized later that this is my job, not anyone else's.

You can see that my passivity, stemming partly from a childhood loss, was a kind of emotional dependency in which I expected something or someone—in this case the Marines—to solve my problems for me, to make me feel good about myself, to rescue me. But other unconscious forces were operating in me that also added to my passivity. A part of me was quite depressed and doubted that there *was* a solution to my problems. I didn't have much faith in myself, and I had good reason: it was during my stint in the Marines that my alcoholism and addiction to other drugs became full-blown.

Everything came to a head when I was caught in the airport on a furlough with a bunch of illegal drugs. I was so messed up, I'd walked around the airport hiding my extra stash in ashtrays, all the while being followed by airport police. My arrest ended up being a kind of intervention. Fortunately for me, the people who caught me decided not to arrest me but instead threatened to contact my commander and report what had happened at the airport.

When I arrived at the Kaneohe Marine Corps Air Station, I turned myself in to get help. The Marines had just started an addiction treatment program. So, rather than going to jail or getting a dishonorable discharge, I was put into a military treatment program in Hawaii.

And what a good thing that was! I obviously hadn't done a very good job with my life up until then. I was in a personal crisis, insensitive to my own experience, and still seeking the fairy godmother to set me on the right path. As I look back, it seems like a miracle that this intervention set me on a path where I was eventually able to unravel and heal most of the pain I experienced in my childhood.

Yet, as I embarked on recovery, I still wouldn't tell the people who were trying to guide me that what they were advising wasn't working for me. I wanted them to read my mind because I was afraid of asserting myself and alienating them. As one of my patients eloquently put it, "I didn't have a speaking part in my own life." When it came to speaking to people on a more intimate level, I remained mute.

However, I was fortunate in treatment to get a very fine sponsor, Tom, to challenge and guide me. At first I wasn't ready to give up my passivity and admit that recovery was *my* responsibility. I couldn't see my passivity, but Tom could sense that I was too dependent on him for my recovery. He knew he had to do something to help me stand on my own two feet. That's because, like most of us alcoholics and addicts, Tom had been passive and dependent, too. Tom's sponsor had seen his emotional dependency and created a situation that forced him to grow by moving away. Tom was devastated, but he learned to stand on his own two feet.

So Tom did something similar for me but in a very different way. He gave me a copy of Sheldon Kopp's book *If You Meet the Buddha on the Road, Kill Him!* It made a significant impact on my attitude toward myself, my relationship with Tom, and my recovery. Kopp's main message is that if we want to experience full enlightenment, we need to stop depending on teachers and gurus—including the Buddha himself! He asserts that enlightenment is a unique experience for each person and eventually has to come from within, not through adopting other people's methods and ideas as your own. We can learn from others and often need the guidance of a teacher, or in my case, a sponsor. But eventually we have to find our own path.

As I dug into the book, I realized that the author was helping me confront that part of myself that was extremely passive and emotionally dependent. I finally faced the fact that a large part of me was still looking for someone to take care of me, to tell me what to feel and believe, what to think and do, and ultimately take responsibility for my recovery. I didn't want to grow up.

This childlike part of me projected the responsibility for my growth and recovery onto my sponsor, my therapist, the meetings I was attending, and even onto the Twelve Step program itself. I was hoping that "they" (whoever *they* were) had the answers for me. Even though I was in AA and trying to work the program, I was psychologically and emotionally dependent upon people or circumstances to improve my lot. I thought that if my life improved, it would be because of *their* advice. But if I didn't get better, then I could blame them. After all, I was following their direction! Needless to say, with this toxic attitude my chances of getting and staying sober were slim to none—and slim was holding a ticket on the next bus out of town.

You can see the pattern—I thought my mother and grandfather should have eased my pain; I thought my father should have been there to help me grow up. I thought the Marines should have made me a man and given me self-esteem. I thought my sponsor, my AA meetings, and my therapist should heal me and make me whole. It was always someone *other* than me who should be in charge of me.

Today, my passivity still rears its ugly head to a certain degree in several areas of my life. But I'm thankful it's not nearly as strong as it was back then. If it were, I truly believe that I wouldn't be sober today.

As I look back, I see that my drinking and using gave me a temporary sense of relief from the prison I created for myself. It allowed me to tolerate the intolerable and live with the unbearable—but at a great price. I lost myself and my integrity. Thanks to the fortuitous "intervention" that led me to the Marines' treatment program, and thanks to my sponsor's insight in giving me that book at just the right time, I began the journey on my own path, which has included working an authentic Twelve Step program that has given me back my integrity and helped me discover and recover my true self.

Finding Your Path in Recovery

So now we know what passivity looks like and how it sabotages recovery. It manifests itself in the belief (insistence, really) that someone else—our sponsor, therapist, or magical fairy godmother—can fix our problem. There's a corollary, too—the belief that there is only one path to recovery, when in fact there are *many*. If we think about it, these two are really the same thing. That all-purpose one path is simply a substitute for the idea that someone will rescue us. This passive approach to recovery stems from our emotional dependency—we feel dependent on something or someone else to make things "right" for us.

Now I'd like to invite you to do a spot-check inventory on yourself, looking at the role that passivity and emotional dependency may be playing in your own life and in your recovery.

If you're honest with yourself, you'll undoubtedly see a certain degree of passivity and emotional dependency. These may be setting you up to believe that if you just follow directions, Good Orderly Directions, you'll be okay. The reality is that you *won't* be okay if you just follow good directions. You need to take total responsibility for your recovery. You need to absorb and integrate what you're learning about yourself, or else it won't become a workable part of your personality. Instead it will remain simply a good idea that came from someone or something else, but will never become a part of who you are.

Now that doesn't mean that following directions is always harmful, because it isn't. You see, there's a paradox operating here. We need to take direction—we need the help of other people. We cannot solve a problem with the same consciousness that created it. But on the other hand, if we follow directions blindly, without looking within to see how those directions apply—or don't apply—to us specifically, they won't do us much good. So what's the balance between accepting outside guidance and passively following direction? *The balance is found when we maintain an attitude that welcomes experimentation.*

Experimentation nourishes recovery and personal maturation. Let's look at a simple analogy. When we shop for clothes, we're experimenting with various colors, styles, and cuts of clothing to see which work for your size and shape and personality. We're trying things on to see how they fit and feel. We can do the same with behaviors and concepts in recovery, and this experimentation is an important part of the process.

But you can't really experiment if you are passive, because you'll be leaving yourself out of the experiment. If you try the clothes on but never look in the mirror to see how you like them, you'll never make a judgment about what works for you. You'll just be wearing the clothes the salesperson told you looked good on you. Similarly, if you just passively follow advice about recovery without trying to determine whether it helps move you along your *own* path, you'll miss the whole benefit of experimentation. You'll fail to take responsibility for your own recovery.

Preparing Yourself for the Recovery Journey

Taking responsibility for our own recovery by experimenting and observing the results sounds great, but we need to be more specific if we're to take it into actual practice. We need to answer these questions:

- What does it really mean to take responsibility?
- What do we need to do to prepare ourselves for the journey?
- How do we know when the results of an experiment are successful, and when they aren't?

We know that passivity and emotional dependency are toxic

to our recovery. If we are to reverse those toxic effects, we need to know where to apply our best efforts.

In the introduction to this book, I mentioned that recovery was like tackling a difficult hike. If you were planning to do that, you'd probably train to ensure that your fitness would support the physical challenges that lie ahead. You'd research the trail and understand its nature as well as possible. You'd pack the supplies necessary to sustain you.

Preparing for the recovery journey requires a different kind of training: you need to develop the ability to pay attention to and understand your subjective experience. This attention and understanding will help you determine whether your recovery experiments are moving you in a positive or negative direction. This ability has been called *inward searching.* I'll define it in a moment, but first, there's some bad news. This ability has been thwarted throughout our lives by a number of different forces. Addiction is especially good at destroying this capacity.

As addiction progresses, we desensitize ourselves to the fact that we're violating our own values and integrity. We dull our awareness so that we don't experience the incongruence between our behavior and our personal values or integrity. Otherwise, we'd throw ourselves into a state of cognitive and emotional dissonance—an unbearable state of intellectual and emotional pain and anxiety. We humans are hardwired to avoid this internal dissonance, so we pretend that what is wrong is right and what is right is wrong. We turn things around to suit our needs and avoid reality. For example, it suddenly becomes okay to steal a little money from our loved ones in order to procure the next fix. After all, we tell ourselves, they've got more than they need, or we know we'll pay it back later. Somewhere inside, a voice is screaming that what we're doing is wrong, but we pretend we don't hear it, so we don't feel the painful dissonance. We do that enough, and eventually we can't even hear the voice. We have dulled our awareness.

To get well, we have to recover our awareness of the voice of our best or true self. We have to develop the ability to turn inward to discover what path is best for us. This ability, as I noted, is called inward searching. It's a process by which we tune our awareness to our subjective experience in the moment and allow it to move in whatever direction it takes (Bugental, 1978). Our inward searching is guided by our concern for our recovery along with our intention to discover our personal truth, or at least to discover new possibilities in our relationship with our problem, with ourselves, and with others.

Inward searching is critical to our journey in recovery. It becomes our compass to help identify our true north. By becoming thoughtfully aware of our subjective experience, we learn to identify whether something is nourishing or toxic to our recovery. This awareness guides us on our recovery journey, but only if we're listening to our true selves. If experimenting is how we take responsibility for our recovery—rather than being passive and emotionally dependent—inward searching is how we find out if our experiments are working. Just as we experiment with clothes and look in the mirror to make a judgment, we experiment with concepts and behaviors and look inward and engage our subjective experience to make a judgment.

To check in with your inner self this way, you need to *be present* to your experience. Being present is a result of being aware of what you are experiencing in this moment, and seeing how this moment moves to the next moment. This means listening to your body as well as your thoughts. Often your mind expresses itself through body sensations. As you learn to listen to yourself and understand what those sensations are telling you, you learn deeper truths about yourself and your feelings. So when you tune in to yourself and take your present body-mind experience into account, you can better know if you're on the right path. You'll find yourself moving toward fulfilling a need, expressing a heartfelt desire, mobilizing yourself to realize a dream, or moving toward completing some unfinished business.

There is a force within each of us that creates a psychological imperative to move in the direction that will make us more complete, more whole, and closer to realizing our potentialities. Inward searching helps resensitize us to that imperative.

So be still, and take the time to listen to yourself. Meditation and especially mindfulness practices are a great way to practice this important faculty. You can learn more about these practices at the Mindful website (www.mindful.org) and other related sites. Author Thérèse Jacobs-Stewart relates the practice specifically to recovery in her book *Mindfulness and the Twelve Steps: Living Recovery in the Present Moment* (Hazelden, 2010).

Develop an attitude of patient experimentation

When we experiment, we don't know what the outcome will be. That's why it's called an experiment! It's scary to try something that feels so uncertain. We can reduce the fear if we prepare ourselves to tolerate uncertainty and discomfort while we discover the solutions that work best for our particular recovery journey. So when we try something new (whether it's our own idea or one suggested by a sponsor or therapist), we can expect to feel uncomfortable doing the new thing at first. Still, we have to follow through with the experiment and find what meaning might be there, regardless of how it feels at first. This approach is very different from the toxic attitude that says life should be easy and fun. Of course, life *can* be easy and fun at times, but not all the time. Most of us alcoholics and addicts don't want to believe this fact because it doesn't fit with how we thought life should be when we were using—easy and fun, all the time.

Life is what it is. What matters is how we cope with it (Satir, 1972). Demanding that life conform to our expectations undermines our ability to cope. As I often tell my clients, the "problem" you face is never the real problem. The *real* problem is *how you are coping* with the "problem."

So when we experiment, we need to notice whether we're learning to cope with life on *life's* terms, not holding out for some fairy-godmother expectations. This will help us develop emotional sobriety in addition to our physical sobriety. In other words, rather than depending on someone or something else for our recovery, we will depend on our inner wisdom to help us determine whether our experiments move us forward or backward.

Watch your attitude for signs of rigidity

If we believe that once we find the path that seems to work, it will *always* work for us, we're setting ourselves up for failure. A healthy recovery is flexible. It allows us to alter our efforts according to our needs.

It's like managing a condition such as asthma, which I suffer from. There are times when I don't need to take medication to manage this chronic illness. I am breathing just fine. Other times I might need to take a puff or two of my inhaler, especially when I exercise. If there is a high pollen count in the air, I might need to take my medication daily, sometimes twice a day if the allergens are really bad. If I get a respiratory infection from a cold or the flu, then I might need to use several medications to restore normal breathing. If things get really bad, I need to be admitted to the hospital.

I would describe my efforts in recovery similarly. In early recovery I attended AA meetings daily, worked with a therapist, attended growth groups, spent as much time as I could with my sponsor, exercised, hung out with sober friends, got involved with service, and worked the Steps. After my first year I attended two to four meetings per week and continued with therapy, but I spent less time with my sponsor, only talking with him about once every other week.

Over the past forty-four years, my recovery has been different at different times, depending on what I needed to do to manage my addiction. Sometimes I need to attend a meeting every day; at other times I don't attend many meetings. There have been times when I've needed psychotherapy or marriage counseling, and times when I've needed a week of daily meetings with my sponsor. We adjust our recovery path to fit our current needs, and these will always change.

Rigidity and intolerance are toxic to our growth in recovery. Rigidity can sometimes seem to us like a responsible action, since we're very carefully following some prescribed path. That's not passive, right? It seems like we're *doing something*. But rigidity is really just another way of being passive—we're letting the "path" tell us where to go, rather than evaluating our circumstances, looking inward, and determining what we need next in life.

Rigidity, intolerance, passivity, emotional dependency—they are part of the same messy nest of unproductive attitudes that limit our growth and thwart our ability to deal with life on life's terms. Real strength and responsible action grow from flexibility and humility, not rigidity. The more flexible and humble our behavior, the better we can cope, meet our needs, and respond respectfully to the needs of others.

Summary: How Do We Know If We're on the Right Path?

As you experiment with new ideas, and patiently notice your feelings as you do so, you'll start to learn whether you're on the right path. Your answers to these questions will tell you whether what you're doing is nourishing or toxic to you and your recovery.

- Has your obsession with alcohol and other drugs been lifted?
- Are you striving to develop the best possible attitude toward your problems, yourself, and others?
- Are you open-minded and willing to experiment?
- Can you tolerate seeing yourself as you are—and can you begin striving to be what you can be?
- Do you make amends to those you've hurt, trying to make restitution or otherwise repair the harm you've caused?
- Do you openly share with others what you've learned in recovery?
- Do you admit when you make a mistake and strive to learn from it?
- Are you more invested in being who you are—and less driven by the desire for success and having things?

What were your answers? If you're on the right path, your life will be vibrating with vitality. In sum, if you are on the right path, you will know it by the quality of your life.

When we follow a path that is nourishing, we have the freedom to experience ourselves and our world in our own way (Greenwald, 1977). We stand for ourselves but not against anyone. We're clear about who we are and what we want, but we're not rigid. We change with time and circumstance. We strive to be compassionate and honest. We cooperate with those we love but don't lose ourselves in the connection.

If the path we're on is right for us, it creates exhilaration and excitement, and fosters a positive attitude toward ourselves, others, and the world in which we live. It encourages feelings of love, contentment, joy, and creativity.

In conclusion, it doesn't really matter what you do to get sober and stay sober, as long as you're honest with yourself about the results. The right path will reveal itself to you as you check in with and become aware of your inner experience. If you sincerely want to get and stay sober, then find the courage to go to any lengths to find a solution.

In the next chapter we'll further explore the differences between passivity and acceptance.

Stupid Thing 2

Conning Yourself by Labeling Passivity as "Acceptance and Surrender"

Passivity means letting things happen without claiming our role in events. Real acceptance and surrender involve actively taking responsibility for the things we can change and accepting the things we cannot.

When I met Jeff, he'd been attending AA meetings, dutifully following his sponsor's advice, and trying to stay sober for about two years. He was in his mid-thirties and quite despondent. He just couldn't figure out what real sobriety meant. He'd string together a few dry weeks and then drink again. Although he was single, he very much wanted a relationship. He admitted that his drinking had sabotaged every previous serious relationship, and he knew he needed to get sober to have a chance at the life he wanted.

So what was missing from Jeff's program? What kept him from moving forward? As you will see, Jeff was conning himself. He claimed to surrender to the disease and accept that he was an alcoholic, but he really was only passively submitting to a program he hadn't fully embraced as his own. Like many other people early in recovery, Jeff was suffering from an unstated internal conflict that caused him to deceive himself. Let's get back to his story to see how it played out.

Jeff explained to me that he was attending up to five meetings a week and spending time with a solid group of men who were involved in their AA programs. He also had a reliable sponsor who was very committed to helping others. The sponsor spent a lot of time with Jeff, and for the most part Jeff followed his sponsor's direction.

Despite this good direction and support, Jeff struggled. He'd get thirty days and then relapse. He'd get forty-five days, then drink again. The pattern repeated over and over, and he'd never pieced together more than sixty days of sobriety.

As we talked, I kept asking myself, "What's missing from Jeff's program? What's Jeff doing that's keeping him from staying sober?" I asked Jeff what he understood about his problem staying sober. He said that he didn't know: "I'm baffled. I do everything my sponsor tells me to do, but to no avail."

Jeff's response was revealing; it suggested to me that he was passive in his recovery.

Here's what I know about recovery: *our results will be proportionate to our level of commitment and effort.* If we approach recovery with less than a rigorous effort, we probably won't get the change we desire. Jeff was following directions and doing what his sponsor said, but he was doing so passively. He wasn't putting his all into it. My job with Jeff, I saw, would be to help him first become aware that he was passive and then to become aware of what was *causing* his passivity.

Later in this same session I discovered that Jeff had doubts about never drinking again. But he wouldn't discuss his doubts with his sponsor, because he feared his sponsor wouldn't want to keep working with him. Jeff had kept these thoughts to himself—which meant he wasn't being completely honest with his sponsor. He went on to say that the reason for those doubts was that his job as a salesman required him to entertain high-powered clients. He was afraid that he wouldn't be much fun or interesting sober, and that he'd lose their accounts.

Do you see a theme here? Jeff was too concerned about how he was going to be perceived. He was worried that his sponsor wouldn't want to work with him if he shared how he really felt, and that clients wouldn't want to work with him because he wasn't any fun when he wasn't drinking. He didn't think he was good enough. He had to act like someone he thought he *should* be depending on the circumstance.

Jeff soon revealed another important concern: he felt some social anxiety when he was sober, and alcohol loosened him up. He could be silly or outrageous, as the situation dictated. His drinking helped him to act contrary to his real feelings. Jeff had become psychologically dependent on the alcohol to help him function better in demanding social situations with clients. He was terrified that if he were sober, his social anxiety would get the better of him.

Now we were getting down to the causes and conditions that were responsible for his relapses. Deep inside, Jeff was conflicted about whether he should quit drinking, and he was avoiding this conflict by conning both himself and his sponsor. Following the lead of others in his group, he *said* he'd surrendered and accepted his need for help. But he secretly held a major reservation about sobriety, one that he didn't dare share with his sponsor (or with anyone else in the fellowship).

In practice, this meant that on several counts Jeff appeared to be a model of recovery! He attended the meetings he was supposed to attend. He did the writing assignments he was asked to do. He showed up when he was told to show up. But he didn't tell his sponsor about his conflicted feelings. The result of this deception was his predictable, continual pattern of relapses. Without rigorous honesty, Jeff was unable to stay sober.

Jeff's feelings and experience aren't unusual—most of us are conflicted about being sober. We struggle with some form of passivity, typically avoiding personal responsibility for finding our way in recovery. Passivity and avoidance wield their toxic influence in a variety of ways.

Our unwillingness to accept full responsibility for ourselves is a manifestation of our lack of commitment. Believing that we can show up to recovery without experiencing internal conflict is a sure sign that our commitment isn't what it needs to be. It's a myth that recovery, or any kind of meaningful change, can be conflict-free. Internal conflict doesn't indicate that something is wrong with us. Rather, it is a signal that an issue needs to be resolved between what we *think* we should do and how we actually feel.

UCLA psychologist Jerry Greenwald focused his work on the toxic beliefs that sabotage our lives. This meant that he understood conflict deeply. In his words:

> Conflict is a normal human process that can best be described as a state of tension or ambivalence we experience in the center of our emotional lives and feel primarily in the chest and stomach. When faced with the need to make a decision, we usually try to weigh the facts rationally (our cortex is not unlike a computer) and determine what we "should do." The trouble is that intellectual decisions do not necessarily alter our emotional (body) feelings. When the two are at odds, as is quite common, particularly in our personal lives where emotions play a greater role, the conflict remains and may be heightened by our efforts to shove an intellectual decision down our physical throats. (1977, p. 24)

And that was Jeff's dilemma. Intellectually he thought he should be able to control his drinking, while emotionally he knew he couldn't and that his drinking was causing him serious trouble. But he couldn't be straight about the conflict with his sponsor because he thought he shouldn't be conflicted.

I've seen this pattern often in my practice. Clients have reservations about staying sober, or they're ambivalent about some other issue espoused by the counselor, sponsor, therapist, or philosophy of the program they're attending. But it's hard to be honest, because they "shouldn't feel this way." These folks do not share their truth because they believe it would be inappropriate or unacceptable.

Of course, in some situations these clients' hidden feelings *would* be labeled as inappropriate by some. They might be shamed by their family, society, or even some members of their peer support group. It can be risky to tell the truth. There is much rigidity in our culture and in some recovery programs, whether they're based on the Twelve Steps or on another philosophy.

But here's the dilemma that this passivity and dishonesty creates. If we're not completely honest, then we will never get the help we need to resolve our conflict. *Full recovery means finding the courage to take a risk and doing what is uncomfortable, to speak up, especially when we don't want to.*

To fully commit to recovery means that we directly address our internal conflict. *Conflict does not mean something is wrong with us.* Conflict reflects the fact that we are often of two minds about a decision. To resolve the conflict, we need to respect both sides of ourselves so we can integrate the differences and then act wholeheartedly.

That's one of the biggest mistakes I see people make in their recovery. Just like Jeff, they're afraid to fully experience and own their conflict. So they con themselves and others, pretending they've surrendered to their problem and accepted their recovery program.

They therefore *appear* to be "following the rules." But they're just papering over an internal conflict they're afraid to admit to. It shouldn't surprise us that this happens—after all, to surrender and accept does connote "giving in and going along," which to some ears sounds like passive submission. But in the context of working a rigorous Twelve Step or other abstinence-based recovery program, surrender and acceptance are *not* passive and don't condone inaction.

They are, in fact, actions.

Understanding Surrender and Acceptance

To see just how the concepts of surrender and acceptance differ from passivity and compliance, let's turn to the writings of psychiatrist Harry Tiebout, a good friend to the early fellowship of Alcoholics Anonymous. Tiebout developed a close friendship and therapeutic relationship with Bill Wilson and also treated several members of the new fellowship—work that led to many important observations about the psychological characteristics of alcoholics and the process of recovery.

Tiebout made an important distinction between *submission* or compliance (both of which are characterized by passivity) and *surrender* or true acceptance. "In submission, an individual accepts reality consciously, but not unconsciously," he said. "With submission, which is at best a superficial yielding, tension continues." In other words, the person is still in conflict about the decision not to drink (Tiebout, 1999).

This tension was evident in Jeff. He wasn't sure if quitting drinking was the right thing for him to do, but he sure wasn't admitting this conflict to himself or his sponsor. A civil war was raging inside him; it was hard to accept that there was a war, and he was afraid of what would happen to him if he surrendered!

Tiebout noted what happens when mere submission becomes true surrender.

> When an individual surrenders, the ability to accept reality functions on the unconscious level, and there is no residual of battle. . . . *It is . . . a moment when the unconscious forces of defiance and grandiosity actually cease to function effectively.* When that happens, the individual is wide open to reality; he or she can listen and learn without conflict and fighting back. . . . It is now possible to define the emotional state of surrender as *a state in which there is a persisting capacity to accept reality.* (Tiebout, 1999, p. 23)

This is an extraordinary insight into the process of submission and surrender. I would add only one observation about the conscious and unconscious. I believe it helps us take personal responsibility if we distinguish between what we want to be aware of and what we don't want to be aware of. The former we experience as *conscious* and the latter we label as *unconscious*—but we are ultimately responsible for both. What we often label as unconscious is more accurately called *pre*conscious: we have some awareness of it but won't allow it to come to full consciousness—and thus we avoid acting on it.

I make this distinction because I think it's more empowering to consider parallel states of consciousness rather than hierarchical ones. I take much more responsibility when I own that there are certain things that I don't want to admit about myself and other things that I readily admit and accept about myself.

So in the case of Jeff, he hadn't fully let into his consciousness the growing evidence that he couldn't control his drinking and his growing fears about the impact of quitting alcohol. He kept that awareness in the background. Jeff didn't want to accept that his drinking was out of control, that he was an alcoholic.

With the real conflict out in the open, Jeff and I focused our efforts on resolving this conflict. To this end, I asked him to have a dialogue between the part of him that wanted to keep drinking and the part of him that wanted to stop. Here's a snapshot of what happened:

> *Keep-Drinking Jeff:* I'm afraid we'll fall flat on our face at social events. We're boring without alcohol, but when we drink we're the life of the party. We're funny, silly, and outrageous, and our clients love being with us because we're so entertaining.
>
> *Stop-Drinking Jeff:* Look, I don't like our job that much anyway, so it may be time to change careers. And I don't like the price we've paid for drinking. We can't keep a serious relationship going. Jane left because she just didn't want to put up with our drinking, and we really loved her.
>
> *Keep-Drinking Jeff:* Change careers? Are you serious? Where else are we going to make that kind of money? We love our lifestyle and the fact that we can do whatever we want to do. Our drinking hasn't been as bad as most of what we hear about in meetings.
>
> *Stop-Drinking Jeff:* That doesn't mean our drinking isn't going to get that bad. Remember what they say: it hasn't happened *yet!*
>
> *Keep-Drinking Jeff:* Sounds like brainwashing to me. Those AA meetings can really be full of nonsense.

As I listened to Jeff's internal dialogue, it became obvious that neither side was really hearing or addressing the concerns of the other. This kept Jeff locked in the conflict with no end in sight.

I made Jeff aware of what was happening, and he suddenly started to cry. "I just realized that I have no faith in myself to be okay without drinking," he said. "It's like I've given up on myself. I don't believe I can change and mature. Wow, that sucks!"

This awareness propelled Jeff into a much more active role in his recovery. He started to openly share his ambivalence in meetings and was surprised at how many people told him afterward that they'd had similar feelings but were afraid to share them with the group. So not only did Jeff set himself free from his passivity, he also unshackled several other people in the meetings.

To establish a solid foundation for our recovery, we must take a *therapeutic stance,* which means stating what is true for us and facing our conflicts. This is what acceptance and surrender really mean: we cope with what is, rather than get lost in what we think things should be like or how other people want us to be. We mobilize ourselves to be honest about where we are, rather than trying to be somewhere or someone we are not. In Jeff's case, speaking his truth meant he was honest with himself, his group, and his sponsor about his internal conflict. He quit saying he'd "accepted and surrendered" to his alcohol addiction and admitted that he wasn't sure. Paradoxically, this admission readied him to truly accept his condition. The admission was an act of taking responsibility rather than passive compliance. And rather than rejecting him (as he'd feared), his group and sponsor embraced him.

If you're being passive in your recovery, own it. Declare that you are being passive. But if you *really* want to have a different experience, then take a risk and have a dialogue with the passive part of your personality, as Jeff did. Try to understand this part of yourself.

See what you can do to support it so that it becomes willing to take some risks and support *you* in mobilizing yourself.

Whenever you have trouble accepting something about yourself, explore your resistance. I'd suggest doing some incomplete sentence work. Take each of the following incomplete sentences and write them on a fresh page: onscreen or on paper, either way. Then say the sentence out loud and write down the first response that comes to mind. Keep repeating the root of the sentence and writing your response until you say the sentence and nothing more comes to mind. As you respond to each sentence, become aware of how you are feeling.

- If my passivity could talk, it would say . . . .
- Passivity benefits me by . . . .
- The hardest thing about mobilizing myself to create the life I want is . . . .
- I refuse to accept . . . .
- If I accept that I am unable to control my drinking or using, it would mean that . . . .
- If I were to accept my addiction, the idea I'd have to give up about myself is . . . .
- The hardest thing about accepting my addiction is . . . .
- What I might feel if I finally accept and surrender to my addiction is . . . .
- Surrender could empower me by . . . .

Have some fun with these things. Another toxic myth is that in order to grow up we must be serious. Nonsense. Recovery doesn't have to always be heavy—we can have fun along the way. There's a time to be serious, but we also need to learn to laugh at our grandiosity and deviance and the insanity of addiction.

Summary: It's Time to Get Angry at Yourself

If none of these suggestions have worked to help you move beyond your passivity, then maybe it's time to get angry with yourself. Why? When nothing works, it often means that you're giving up on yourself. Your passivity is so entrenched that it's saying you *can't* change, you *have to* settle for failure, for a life half-lived. I simply don't believe this. You don't have to let this part of you continue to control your life. I believe we have an incredible growth force within us that is readily available to empower our lives. Your job is to release it by weakening the destructive force of passivity. You have no concept of your potential until you experiment with some new possibilities.

Passivity is destructive to recovery. We need to mobilize all our sincerity, all our resourcefulness, and all the best in ourselves in order to recover from addiction. Genuine acceptance and surrender is the result of a lot of hard work that comes from facing who we are and who we are not. Don't shy away from this work; you are laying a foundation for the rest of your life.

In the next chapter we'll keep exploring how passivity undermines our full recovery.

Stupid Thing 3

Confusing Meeting Attendance with Working a Program

We call it working *a program because it takes effort! Simply sitting at a meeting is too passive. Confronting yourself, striving to have the best possible attitude, finding the right help or the right sponsor, and actively practicing the Steps is what matters.*

If you attend a Twelve Step recovery program, you've probably been advised to go to ninety meetings in ninety days (or at least heard someone being given this advice). Patients who finish a thirty- to ninety-day inpatient program are typically given an aftercare plan that includes that direction. I've even seen addiction counselors working in an outpatient or day treatment program give their patients the prescription of ninety meetings in ninety days.

This advice has been offered as a remedy for many ailments encountered in recovery:

- If you relapse, go to ninety meetings in ninety days.
- If you're depressed or anxious, attend ninety meetings in ninety days.

- If you're having marital problems, you definitely need ninety meetings in ninety days.
- If you're having trouble at work, go to ninety meetings in ninety days.
- If you're thinking about a drink or using, guess what—you should go to ninety meetings in ninety days.

I've always felt that there was something missing in this advice. Of course, I see value in attending meetings: they play an important part in recovery. AA and NA (Narcotics Anonymous) meetings saved my life back in 1971, when I returned to the States from Vietnam. We often hear something in a meeting that helps us gain perspective on the Steps and on living a sober lifestyle. Meetings can also be a refuge where the support of other alcoholics and addicts is an invaluable part of our ongoing recovery. So there is no question that there is a time and place in recovery for making meeting attendance a priority. But there's still something lacking in this advice.

You see, this advice says nothing about *how* we need to show up when we're sitting in a meeting. Attending meetings without some direction is another way that we approach recovery passively, rather than taking an active role in our sobriety. Again, in Earnie Larsen's words: "Your program cannot take you further than your own definition of recovery" (1985, p. 11). If we don't define what recovery means to us, we are less likely to get what we need. Showing up at a lot of meetings without a plan is too happenstance for those of us who are serious about developing a new way of life. Sure, some good things come from luck, but many more good things will come to you if you have a plan that takes into account your specific needs and goals.

Your personal definition of recovery is the lynchpin of your plan. That definition will help you focus your energy and effort to grow along emotional and spiritual lines. So take a moment and think about what you want recovery to mean for you and your life. This definition, of course, will depend on where you are in your trek. Early on you may be concerned principally with just staying sober, and rightfully so. But once you're stabilized and not dealing with the obsessions or cravings, you can start to focus on the broader problems of living a sober lifestyle. Therefore, we attend meetings and work the Steps with these goals:

- expand our consciousness
- become more emotionally mature
- continue to heal our relationships
- improve conscious contact with our Higher Power
- be of service to others
- learn how to "practice these principles in all our affairs"

When we attend meetings passively, we can fail to find these important recovery lessons—even when we *appear* to be doing the right things. That's the big risk in the "ninety meetings in ninety days" solution: it looks good, but we're missing the full benefits of recovery. Worse, we can be deceiving ourselves.

Let's look at an example of how passivity sabotaged both a recovery and a relationship. I want you to meet Louise, an AA member and the wife of my client John. Louise seemed to be working a great program. The key word is *seemed* because, as you'll see, she resisted doing some important emotional work that would have made a huge difference in her recovery and in her relationships with her husband and fellow AA members.

Louise attended upward of four meetings a week, volunteered to serve as a panel speaker, had a sponsor, and even sponsored several women. Her recovery looks good when I describe it here, doesn't it? But please suspend your judgment until I tell you more about how Louise was dealing with her struggles with her husband and her children.

Louise had relapsed a couple of times during the past decade, but had also put together several long periods of sobriety, most recently celebrating five years. Anyone in Louise's Twelve Step community would have told you that Louise worked a great program. But the appearance of a good program—attending meetings, spouting the right platitudes, volunteering, and so forth—can be deceptive. It was the negative quality of her most important relationships—rather than her relapses—that tipped me off: Louise's supposed "great program" was masking both passivity and a resistance to change.

Louise and her husband John had been estranged through much of their marriage. Her drinking and his codependency exacerbated their alienation. John had hoped that with sobriety they would finally find each other and become more intimate. But now that Louise was sober, they were still alienated. In many ways, Louise's sobriety was even more painful for John because he could no longer blame the alcohol for their lack of intimacy. Now he knew something else was wrong, and he was committed to finding out what it was.

So upon my request, John invited Louise to one of our sessions. She reluctantly joined us. But as I would soon find out, Louise was only going to attend the sessions if it was on her terms.

After my initial welcome, she quickly assured me that she was there to help her husband clean up his act, because she was getting the help she needed from the AA program. "I don't need therapy. AA is giving me everything I need to stay sober," she declared.

She went on to give me her diagnosis of what was wrong in their marriage. "It's his attitude. He's never satisfied with anything I do and criticizes me all the time." John chimed in and said he felt the same way—that he could do nothing right as well. Louise countered that she was sick of John's asking her to talk about their relationship. For her, there was nothing to talk about. She was working her program, he should work his, and that was that.

I pointed out to Louise that her position put her husband between a rock and a hard place. "So you don't want John to discuss his frustration or grievances about the marriage with you?"

She didn't hesitate. "No. He should go and talk to his sponsor. I am not his sponsor."

I told her that it seemed like she didn't want to be his wife, let alone his sponsor. She glared at me with disdain. Clearly she didn't like that observation!

When I asked her husband to comment on her idea of how things were supposed to be in the marriage, he said that her attitude left him frustrated and hurt. He'd hoped they could discuss their issues and resolve their differences. "I'm tired of being put off by her and being ridiculed for wanting a relationship," he added.

Louise quickly reacted and told John that this wasn't her problem, it was his. As we continued our discussion, I learned that Louise's sharp tongue had also alienated her from her four children, who had actively encouraged their father to get a divorce. Trust me, this isn't normal. Children don't campaign for one parent to divorce the other unless there is some real trouble at home.

Still, I'm not blaming all of their marital problems on Louise. It takes two hands to sink the ship, and John played his role in their problems, too. But the focus here is on Louise, who was supposedly "working a good program." Though she was physically sober, she was not emotionally sober. What do I mean by this?

Louise's physical sobriety had saved her from the immediate crisis of her addiction, but she hadn't done what it took to find emotional sobriety. Louise's need to control her husband and children in order to feel good about herself was a sign of her emotional immaturity. Her acid tongue, tendency to blame others, and refusal to address relationship problems with her husband and children were ample evidence that she was afraid to make a real connection with the people who cared about her, and she dealt with that fear by trying to control them. She believed that everything would be okay if her husband and children unquestioningly obeyed her demands. But she ended up alienating them and creating a toxic atmosphere in the family.

Because the children never learned from their father how to hold on to themselves—that is, not cave in—when their mother was being demanding, they were stuck using the same strategies that their parents modeled for them. Sometimes they were also demanding, sometimes they blamed themselves, sometimes they rebelled, and often they emotionally distanced themselves from the toxic climate in the family. They were doing just what they had learned from Mom and Dad.

If Louise were really working an effective program, she would have been more aware of and admitted her shortcomings. She'd have been willing to address her character defects and change her behavior. She wouldn't have needed to deflect or dismiss her husband's concerns because she would have recognized the behaviors that alienated him and been willing to make amends, trust her Higher Power, and act out of her best self. But she wasn't willing to face her shortcomings. She remained a passive participant in her program, expecting others to change in order for her to be happy. As we spoke further, I learned that in recovery, Louise had fired several of her sponsors because they challenged her. I asked Louise to share with me her definition of recovery. She defined recovery as staying sober, going to meetings, and helping others—that was it. Nothing else!

Her definition of recovery was convenient for her. It let her off the hook. She didn't have to take an inventory, make amends, promptly admit when she was wrong, trust a Power greater than herself, and strive to truly serve others by recognizing the legitimacy of their needs. Her definition of recovery was narrow indeed—but by her definition, she was working a good program.

When we resist seeing something that's obvious to everyone else, it usually means that we're unable to tolerate the truth. We refuse to see who we really are because we're afraid of what we'd see. In this case, Louise would turn the same harsh and blaming attitude on herself that she put on others. As it turned out, she resisted being honest with herself because she would have to admit that her behavior was very similar to her mother's—whom she hated. She had declared early in life that she would never act like her mother—but now she was doing just that, and she was using the program to deflect responsibility for her inappropriate behavior. In her mind, "working a good program" by attending meetings and saying all the right things made her right and anyone who challenged her wrong.

She was unable to admit her wrongs against her children, husband, and others, and seek to make amends. Though no longer drinking, Louise was a classic example of the "dry drunk"—the person who, though sober, refuses to change at a deeper level and continues to inflict pain on oneself and others. The dry drunk misses the full benefits of a rigorous recovery program that addresses their specific needs and is, therefore, always just a sip away from relapse. Louise was selling herself short.

Earnie Larsen explained the problem in this way:

> Victims of dry drunks have made a First Step relative to their addiction, but have not made a First Step relative to the living problems that underlie all addictions and ultimately limit their ability to function in loving relationships. (1985, p. 14)

Louise's problem is not uncommon. Her story illustrates that to get sober and stay sober we need to build a solid foundation for a new way of life that includes finding emotional sobriety. This foundation for recovery rests on the bedrock of humility and is built, block by block, by learning how to be intimate and function in healthy relationships.

Many people who are in trouble go to meetings and just sit there. They don't share. They don't become vulnerable. They don't ask for help or let anyone know that they're in trouble. They don't share that they feel lost or scared. They don't ask for what they need. They may, like Louise, comply with program expectations on the outside, but inwardly they sit and hope that the recovery fairy godmother will come along, wave her magic wand, and make everything okay.

This need to engage in meetings flies in the face of program dogma in some circles—dogma that holds that all you have to do is show up and "act as if" until the miracle happens. It's my experience that miracles *do* happen—to those who are intensely involved in their recovery, rather than passively waiting for change. If we don't face our basic flaws in any focused, consistent, or systematic manner, we will continue to suffer the consequences of our denial and inaction: "sober suffering," in the words of Fred Holmquist, director of the Dan Anderson Renewal Center at the Lodge at Hazelden. Sober suffering springs from the pain and frustration of not knowing how to cope with what is. That's what subjects us to the dry drunk syndrome (Larsen, 1985). And that's what Louise was experiencing: she was sober and she "worked a great program" but continued to exhibit the anger, resentment, and emotional dependency typical of the alcohol- or drug-addicted person.

You cannot get and stay sober by being passive. Recovery requires all hands on deck. All of you—mind, body, and spirit—must show up and get involved if you are going to right the ship.

So why do we remain passive when it's so self-destructive? I believe it's because there are many payoffs for being passive.

- Passivity allows us to collect evidence as to why our life will never work. It allows us to blame someone else for our failure to get and stay sober.
- Passivity allows us to justify a belief that, when we do fail, AA or NA doesn't work for us. While it's true that AA or NA may *not* be a fit for everyone, we won't know unless we actively participate in the process.
- Passivity also allows us to justify the belief that therapy won't work for us. Well, it may *not,* but we won't know unless we become rigorously honest with our therapist.
- Passivity allows us to conclude that sponsors can't help us because they just don't understand our situation. They may *not* understand, but if we've never discussed this doubt honestly, how can any sponsor get more attuned to who we are?

You see the pattern. Passivity can have a big payoff, as it allows us to keep doing what we've always done while blaming others. It's risk-free! We don't have to take a chance on change. Instead, we can *pretend* to change without really changing. That's what Louise was doing when she refused to talk with John about their relationship.

Our passivity can eventually create a sense of hopelessness, despair, and pessimism—the natural consequences of the failure to change. But because we don't see that our passivity is keeping us from change—that our choice to be passive is to blame—we externalize and blame others or circumstances for our continued unhappiness.

We can sabotage our recovery in many different ways. And one of the strongest forms of self-sabotage is passivity, typified by the mindless act of "working a great program," such as sitting in meetings without stating what we expect from recovery; without defining what a "great program" that meets those expectations would actually look like. Becoming aware of how passivity harms us is a key to getting and staying sober.

The Kind of Work That Needs to Be Done in Recovery

We need to think of recovery in stages: Earnie Larsen proposed that idea in 1985. Stage I recovery, he believed, was necessarily focused on getting sober. It typically involves detoxification to break the physical bond of addiction and psychological work to break the bonds of the mental dependence on alcohol or other drugs.

Put simply, Stage I recovery requires admitting the nature of our problem. This isn't as easy as it sounds. Many forces are at work within us that don't want us to admit the nature of our problem. Why? Because for whatever reason, admitting our problem is viewed as subtracting something from who we are, rather than adding to who we are. Often gender rules passed down in our family and culture come into play here, too. For example, many men view surrendering or admitting powerlessness as implying they are less of a man, that they have failed. For many women, losing control means losing one's sense of propriety and dignity and, making one less of a woman. Whether we're male or female, the loss of power, control, dignity, or propriety fills us with shame.

When we finally get honest with ourselves and accept the fatal nature of our condition, recognizing the fact that our entire brain has been hijacked, we experience a paradoxical shift in our ability to deal with our addiction. We come to believe that there is a Power greater than our false addict-alcoholic self—a Power we can actively enlist to uncover our true or spiritual self.

Stage II recovery concerns itself with rebuilding the life we saved in Stage I. Larsen explained it with an analogy from medicine. He said that if our leg was shattered and we were given painkillers without fixing the leg, we'd think we were all right—for a while. But once we were taken off the painkillers, we would experience intense pain and realize the limitations they had masked. Sober suffering can help us realize that we've been walking around on the shattered leg of partial recovery.

This is what working a program is about. Working *all* the Steps systematically and actively helps us face the forces within us that interfere with our ability to improve our relationships with ourselves and with others. The Steps, by giving us the insight and strength to reckon with our emotional dependency and false self, help us develop emotional sobriety.

Here's how Earnie Larsen explained it.

> From a recovery standpoint, both chemical dependency and co-dependency have to do with *intimacy* . . . and intimacy issues are always about the ability to function in relationships. (1985, p. 16)

Our emotional immaturity, emotional dependency, and low self-esteem interfere with our ability to function in intimate relationships. We can't have the intimacy necessary for healthy relationships when our unresolved emotional needs dictate unenforceable rules for how others are supposed to behave so that we feel loved or emotionally secure. The result is that we try to control other people. When our sense of love or emotional security is based on controlling other people, we're never going to feel safe or experience true intimacy or adult love. Does this sound like Louise?

To build a healthy foundation for a relationship, you make room for what you want *and* for what the other person wants, where neither party has to always meet the other's expectations. Respecting each other as separate but equally important people with differences and unique needs strengthens your connection rather than disrupting it.

To get to this place takes a lot of work. It takes a lot of soul-searching and rigorous honesty. We need to step outside of our comfort zone and face our false self—who we are not—so that we can become who we really are. And a passive recovery program, where we just show up to meetings and go through the motions of working the Steps, will only keep us stuck at Stage I, even if we are no longer drinking or using.

So where do we need to focus our work? Stage II recovery is about reclaiming our emotional center of gravity. Emotional sobriety comes with actively taking responsibility for our emotional well-being. We no longer let other people define our reality. We are willing to experiment to discover who we truly are and what we want.

Fill in the following incomplete sentences with the first thought that comes to mind.

- One issue I am passive about in my recovery is . . . .
- One thing I don't want to admit about myself and how I treat others is . . . .
- One thing I have trouble talking to my sponsor about is . . . .
- My unenforceable rule demands that my partner or children or friends have to . . . .
- I use the program to avoid . . . .
- If I were more active when I attended meetings, I would . . . .

Summary: Passive No More

We need to actively digest whatever information we receive—in meetings, from our sponsor, or from our loved ones—to see if it applies to our own recovery. When we critically examine what we're learning about ourselves from our inner experience, we can take what works and feels congruent with our true values, and discard what doesn't. We can only do this if, instead of trying to control, please, or evade others, we try to stay connected by respecting our differences and individual needs.

In Stage I recovery we are motivated by pain. Pain caused by the unmanageability of our lives. Pain caused by guilt, shame, and remorse about how we hurt our loved ones and other people who believed in us. And pain from the struggle we are experiencing in breaking the bond of our addiction.

To begin laying the foundation for our new life, we have to "put the plug in the jug." But once we've established our physical sobriety, we need to quickly work on our emotional sobriety. Emotional sobriety is critical to long-term recovery. In Stage II recovery, we begin to examine the remaining toxic beliefs and attitudes of our false self, we become more familiar with our inner addict, we become aware of unhealthy patterns in our relationships, we discover how to be of real value to others, and we move toward taking total responsibility for our lives.

This new direction in our lives releases the constructive forces of our true self so we can grow along spiritual lines. Rather than being motivated by the pain of active addiction, we are now motivated by the desire to grow—to discover new possibilities in who and what we can be.

Getting sober is hard work, but staying sober and living sober are where the real work begins. We confront the emotional and psychological issues that go hand-in-hand with our physical addiction.

In this chapter we further explored how we use a passive approach to recovery to mask our character defects. As soon as we own our recovery by actively using meetings to work a rigorous Twelve Step program, we embark on the path to emotional sobriety and authentic connection with our fellow travelers. To do this, we need to be willing to face and fully understand our addict self, which is what we'll discuss in the next chapter.

Stupid Thing 4

Failing to Understand and Develop a Healthy Relationship with Your Addict or Alcoholic Self

Addiction has changed us in many ways, both physically and mentally. As our illness progressed, we developed an addict or alcoholic self that joined the rest of the selves that populate us. Over time, that self took complete control of our personality. Even now, in recovery, it's still with us. And if we ignore or underestimate that addict or alcoholic self, we're at a high risk for relapse. Our best chance in recovery is to get to know that self and to learn how to coordinate the rest of our selves with it.

In 2015, Disney Pictures released a great film called *Inside Out*. It's a story about an eleven-year-old girl named Riley. She is happily living in Minnesota and playing her favorite sport, hockey, when her life is suddenly uprooted: her family unexpectedly moves to San Francisco for her father's new job. Viewers can relate. We know that any time something significant is either added or subtracted from our lives, be it positive or negative, we will experience stress in adjusting to the change. But this is not just a stressful experience for young Riley. It is also traumatic.

The film follows Riley as she struggles to cope with the trauma she is feeling while adjusting to her new life in San Francisco, which includes dealing with a new school, new friends, a new house in a new city . . . and no hockey. What's interesting about this film is the perspective it takes. We get to go inside Riley's head and see how the different parts of her are reacting to this traumatic situation.

Inside Out reveals how each of us consists of various parts or selves. We configure these parts with the aim of feeling loved, experiencing joy, and being accepted by others. Ultimately we seek to feel a sense of belonging.

The parts of Riley that we are introduced to are five personified emotions—joy, fear, anger, disgust, and sadness—each making a different contribution to how Riley is reacting to and perceiving the events in her life. Because joy has usually been in the foreground of Riley's life, she becomes disorganized when sadness and fear take center stage. Joy had been Riley's predictable way of coping, and when that was no longer relevant, she had to reorganize herself to cope with her new situation. Riley eventually learns a more realistic balance as she adjusts to the dramatic change in her life. The writers and animators have captured her struggle and communicated it in a very creative way that is meaningful to both adults and children.

What I love about this film is that it illustrates the dilemma we all face. We are not of one mind. Each of us consists of many different selves, which we organize around the concept of who we think we should be.

Very early in life many of us make a decision to shift the focus of our personal growth away from self-actualization—the understanding and expression of our truest self, in which all the components of our personality (our "selves") are valued and integrated—toward actualizing a concept of who we *should* be. So we redirect our growth. Our organizing principle is no longer the self that we truly are—it's the self that we think we should be. I've referred to this before as the *idealized self.* We abandon our true self because we believe this new direction in our development would give us the best chance of belonging and being loved. I've explored what this concept means for people recovering from addiction in some depth in my book *12 Smart Things to Do When the Booze and Drugs Are Gone.*

As the psychologist, humanist, and author Rollo May so astutely observed, the self that we become is the one we think will ensure our existence. We become a false self because we think it will ensure our psychological survival; we will magically feel like we belong. We believe that this false self—which is largely based on what we think others want us to be—will protect us from feelings of rejection, inadequacy, separation, and isolation. It would give us emotional security.

We pay a huge price for this shift in our psychic forces. Karen Horney, a psychoanalyst instrumental in founding feminist psychology, noted that the development of the false self is always at the expense of the true self (Horney, 1950, 1991). We lose ourselves to protect ourselves. We lose our authenticity to ensure emotional security. What a crazy paradox!

As we try to become the person we think we should be, we emphasize some personality characteristics (or selves) at the expense of others. We define some of our selves as essential in organizing our personalities. These *essential selves* then reflect who we think we should be.

For example, if you decided you had to please others to ensure your emotional security, then all the parts of yourself that would support this goal would become essential selves: traits such as self-effacement, self-sacrifice, hypervigilance to others' needs, highly regarding the expressed and unexpressed wishes of others, and so on.

Traits that are desirable but nonessential hang out on stage with the essential selves but play a lesser role. Continuing the example, if you organized yourself around people-pleasing, then some of your nonessential selves might be the parts of you that are fearful, resentful, jealous, or anxious. These selves generally are allowed on stage, as they sometimes assist in the goal of creating a people-pleasing personality and rarely get in the way of that goal. But you'd try not to let them be the featured performers in the play you're putting on for other people.

There would also be another set of characteristics that you'd need to disown because they contradict the false self we are trying to create. You'd hold backstage the selves that are assertive, confident, argumentative, honest, forceful, proud, demanding—and any other part that would indicate that you have needs. Those actors would wreck your play about being a perfect people-pleaser, since they reveal that you don't really want to please other people.

The goal of therapy and recovery is to remove the constraints of the false self on the organization of our personality, so that we can begin to coordinate all that we are into a harmonious, working whole self. By freeing the constructive forces of the true self, we become more integrated. We reorganize our personality so that we function better under challenging conditions. We will be flexible and yet solid. We will support ourselves and validate ourselves. We will intuitively know how to soothe ourselves and heal our wounds.

No doubt, as you read, you are recognizing the way the false-self actors perform on your personal stage. Don't feel alone; the problem of the false self is shared, to differing degrees, by almost everyone on the planet. The false self–true self problem comes with living as an individual in a society, where we seek to balance our desire to belong to a group (to be loved and feel safe) with our desire to express our individuality (to be faithful to our own needs and wants).

But this problem becomes much worse when we are addicted to alcohol and other drugs. Let's explore what happens then.

The Addict Self and the Recovery Self

We've noted how brain research has demonstrated that addiction hijacks the brain: that various essential functions of the brain are recruited to support the use and abuse of drugs. Just as the brain physically changes to support the addiction, we also reorganize our personality to support our addiction. As the disease progresses, we eventually develop an alcoholic or addict self that becomes one of the essential selves discussed above. That's what people in Twelve Step meeting rooms mean when they say, "The disease was talking to me today."

The alcoholic or addict self becomes a very powerful voice among the voices of the other selves in our personality. As addiction progresses, it gains even more clout, exercising veto power over the rest of our selves. It becomes the governing self.

The alcoholic or addict self is the manifestation of the disease in our personality. It's the part of us that decides to drink or use regardless of consequences. It drives us to go to any lengths to get high and fights to protect its right to drink or use. When confronted, this addict self turns reality around to create confusion and doubt in others, as an octopus uses ink as a defense. The addict self is scheming, manipulative, and dishonest. Its major purpose is to ensure that it can continue to drink or get high.

When we begin the journey of recovery, another self begins to emerge and vies for a more important position in our personality. This is the *recovery self*, which is a version of our healthy self.

The recovery self is the antithesis of the addict self. It's the part of us that wants a better life and wants us to be the best we can be. This self hangs out onstage with other essential selves, such as the healer, the compassionate self, the wise self, the seeker, and the spiritual self, to name a few. This part of us seeks wholeness, integrity, and meaning. This recovery self will help us *recover* the lost true self, but only if it's well integrated into our personality. If we let it, the recovery self will stay focused and committed to getting well, and to taking whatever action is necessary for our restoration, redemption, and salvation.

As you might expect, the recovery self and addict self are in conflict. Until we do something that helps us reorganize the way we've configured our various selves into a personality, we will keep doing the same thing, expecting better results.

Carl Jung described the powerful results of this kind of psychic reorganization. In a session with Rowland Hazard, a patient who was having trouble getting and staying sober, Jung told him,

> Here and there, once in a while, alcoholics have what are called vital spiritual experiences. . . . They appear to be in the nature of huge emotional displacements and rearrangements. Ideas, emotions, and attitudes which were once the guiding forces of the lives of these men are suddenly cast to one side, and a completely new set of conceptions and motives begin to dominate them. (Alcoholics Anonymous, 2001, p. 27)

Recovery requires us to let go of our old ideas so they can be replaced with new and more effective attitudes and ways of thinking. This shift in our attitude and way of thinking is the aftermath of a reorganization of our personalities. Recovery entails the same "huge emotional displacements and rearrangements," as Jung put it.

So the question becomes, How do I reorganize my personality so that it supports my efforts in recovery—so that my recovery self is actualized? This is a critical question because it speaks to what needs to happen internally to support the decision to get and stay sober. Please take a moment to think about it, then complete these sentences.

- The part of me that is typically in charge is . . . .
- The part of me that I would like to be the chairman of the board is . . . .
- If the best of me was in charge of the rest of me, it would change . . . .

One of the most important things you can do to support your recovery is to become aware of and better understand your addict self.

Understanding the addict self

Once the addict self integrates itself into our personality, it forever becomes a part of who we are. We can never evict it from renting space in our consciousness; we can't remove it from its seat on the proverbial mental committee that presides over our lives. By the time we seek help through the Twelve Steps, treatment, therapy, or some other method, the addict self has ascended to the position of governing self in our personality. It has become chairman of the board.

With some drugs this coup happens quickly, as is the case with those of us who've used cocaine, crystal meth, or opiates. With other drugs it may take longer, as may happen with alcohol or marijuana. Regardless, once the addict self reaches the elite status of chairman of the board, it demands that we organize our lives according to its needs and desires. Everything else is secondary. Any parts of us that object to its reign are overruled or ignored. We compulsively follow its lead. It's as if we've become zombies driven by only one desire—the desire to drink or use. Nothing else matters!

Unfortunately, the part of ourselves that knows right from wrong, the ethical self, is isolated by the addict self and given very little say in what we do. The result is that we end up violating our own personal values and beliefs.

The disappearance of the ethical self is a common theme among parents who have a child suffering from addiction. They'll say, "I don't even recognize my child any longer; addiction has changed her so much that she doesn't respect any of the values I've tried to model and instill in her." Or a partner will say about a spouse, "I just don't recognize my husband. He's not the man I married."

So the addict self turns us into someone antithetical to our true self. Another false self is created that dominates our lives. It's the unpredictable and dangerous Mr. Hyde to our sober Dr. Jekyll. To regain control of our lives, we have to reorganize our personality. We have to put our true self, represented by our recovery self, in charge. But first we have to get to know our addict self. Let's keep these traits in mind.

- The addict self is unreasonable, irrational, and impulsive. It will not be swayed by reason, and it doesn't care about right or wrong when getting and using alcohol or other drugs is involved.
- The addict self is tricky and adept at convincing us and others that everything is all right and that the addict self really doesn't exist. It will patiently lurk in the shadows until it finds the perfect time to convince us that picking up a drink or using is actually a good idea.
- The addict self doesn't care who it hurts. It wants what it wants when it wants it, and it won't let anything stand in its way.

- The addict self is great at solving problems, overcoming any obstacle to drinking or using placed in its way.
- The addict self has a very limited awareness of the seriousness of our condition. It turns mountains into anthills.
- The addict self will camouflage itself well, making others think that it wants to change, when the reality is that it has no intention of doing anything different.
- The addict self is great at reading the motivations and intentions of other people and using this information to manipulate them—especially people who might threaten its ability to drink or use: spouse, parents, other loved ones or relatives, even well-intentioned therapists or medical doctors.
- The addict self is grandiose. It believes that it is special and therefore the same rules and laws that apply to everyone else don't apply to it.
- The addict self is deviant and rebellious in that it isn't open to help and won't let anyone tell it what to do.
- The addict self is as smart as—and often more clever than—the rational, healthy selves, so it's a worthy adversary.

Stop and reflect on these characteristics. Do you recognize your addict self? Can you see how it has taken over your life? Take a moment to write about your addict self. Can you put your finger on when it took over your life? How much control does it have over your life now?

Think of the Twelve Steps of Alcoholics Anonymous. Step One says, "We admitted we were powerless over alcohol—that our lives had become unmanageable." In other words, we have allowed our addict self to take complete control of our lives, with the result that our lives have become unmanageable. It doesn't have to be this way. We can change and put the best of us in charge of the rest of us. But we need to be willing to go to any lengths to effect this reorganization of our personality.

Let's continue to get to know the addict self. Do the following exercise and see what you learn. Read each of the incomplete sentences below and write down the first thought that comes to mind. Then take a second and third pass through the list, writing down your subsequent thoughts.

- One thing that my addict self doesn't want anyone to know is . . . .
- The addict self in me has planned (or is planning) to sabotage my recovery by . . . .
- The payoff I've gotten for having my addict self run the show is . . . .
- My addict self's behavior is saying that I am . . . .
- To accept that I have a serious problem with alcohol or other drugs, I had to (or have to) give up the idea that I am . . . .
- The addict in me has planned (or is planning) to defeat all efforts to help me by . . . .
- When I ran into trouble because of my drinking or using is, my addict self told me . . . .

Your answers will start to give you some idea of how your addict self thinks and behaves. Now let's find out more about your recovery self.

Getting to know your recovery self

Before we became sober and entered recovery, our recovery self was more potential than actual. We all have potential essential selves: a compassionate self, a spiritual self, a wise self, and so on. But they get buried and overruled by the addict self. Now let's get to know the recovery self. Before we got sober and entered recovery, the recovery self was more of a potential self. It's only when we began our journey in recovery that it began to grow into an essential self—one that can reawaken and coordinate the other potential selves to support your healthy, true self as an integrated personality.

The recovery self is important because it's the intervention of this self that can restore order and balance to our lives. This part of us will accept help and admit that we need it. This part of us is flexible and willing to experiment with different ways of coping. It knows that accepting our limitations and learning to live with them doesn't subtract from but rather adds to who we are. This part of us is grounded in humility and is concerned with building our character. It is not interested in having but rather in being. This part of us does the right thing because it's the right thing to do. The recovery self is committed to resolving differences and to being of value to others. It knows that "we can accomplish together what I cannot accomplish alone."

When our motivation is grounded in our recovery self, we strive to grow. This growth-based motivation is a new development for us. It's different from the motivation of our lower self, which is based on avoiding pain or correcting a deficit. The motivation of our recovery self is robust and not easily diminished by setbacks or lapses. It works with our resilient self so that if we lose our balance, we regain it quickly. Our recovery self marshals our healthy and wise selves to challenge the addict self when it tells us that we're not ready for sobriety. All these selves know we have been in trouble for quite some time and need help. They tell us that enough is enough. It's time to stop the insanity.

But just to *know* we need help isn't enough to override the influence of the addict self. We must continue to nourish and strengthen our recovery self at all stages. You can begin by asking yourself, *Is what I'm doing going to respect and honor my true self?* Good question, but how will we know the answer? Here are a few tips. We are nurturing and honoring our true self when we:

- promptly make amends for something we have done wrong
- admit and accept our limitations
- strive to be authentic and honest
- challenge our emotional dependency and learn to stand on our own two feet
- serve others
- learn from our experience or mistakes
- pressure ourselves to change rather than expect everyone else to change
- deal with life on life's terms

You are starting to see that our recovery self leads us to rediscover our lost true self. So it is imperative that we get to know your recovery self.

Here's another set of incomplete sentences. As before, write the first thought that comes to mind. After you've done this once, repeat the exercise a few more times.

- What I know to be true about my addiction is . . . .
- The most painful thing about being an addict or an alcoholic is . . . .

- To stop listening to what my addict self tells me, one thing I can do is . . . .
- The most important reason to stay sober is . . . .
- When my addict self tells me to drink or get high, one thing I can tell it is . . . .
- To stop obeying my addict self, I have to . . . .
- To neutralize a desire to drink or use, I need to remind myself . . . .
- My recovery self wants me to . . . .

These are just a few of the ways you can begin to give this part of you more of a voice in your life. So get to know your recovery self. It is going to save your life and be the backbone of your recovery.

Addict Self/Recovery Self: A Dialogue

Becoming aware of the relationship that exists between the addict self and recovery self is one key to recovery. Once you become aware of your interactions with these parts of yourself, you can determine whether they're out of balance and toxic to your recovery, or in balance and nourishing to your recovery. If this interaction is toxic, then it's critical that you do something to change it.

To help my clients explore the interrelationship between the addict self and recovery self, I often suggest they act out an internal dialogue. In my office, I place two empty chairs facing each other; their recovery self is imagined sitting in one chair, while their addict self occupies the other. The client shuttles between the two, speaking the dialogue out loud.

As the client externalizes the internal conflict, it becomes clearer what's causing it and what can be done about it. Our addiction can only exist if we obey the addict self or fail to effectively deal with it and what it tells us to do. This exercise helps expose the imbalances and reveal what we can do differently.

So here's an experiment I'd like you to do. Imagine two empty chairs facing each other, and then put your recovery self in one of those chairs and your addict self in the other. Take a moment and see how they look. What differences do you notice between these two parts of yourself? Pay attention to the different types of energy that they emanate. How do you feel when you look at them? Put words on your reactions to each part, such as enticing, scary, appealing, ugly, and so on.

Next imagine them talking to each other. Who speaks first? What does that part say to the other part? How does the other part respond? Let the dialogue unfold for a while. Is the discussion productive or unproductive? Who holds the power in the conversation? Let it evolve some more. What direction does it take? How does the recovery self deal with the addict self? Again, which self appears to have the power? What does the part with the power do to get and sustain that power?

Play around with exaggerating one or both parts. If your addict self says it won't listen to the recovery self, then exaggerate its position. Say something like, "I will never listen to what you or what anyone else says about me. I just won't let myself care about how you feel!" How does the recovery self respond to the addict self when it becomes more outrageous? Then experiment with responding in kind. Your recovery self might say something like, "You don't have to listen to me, and I'm not listening to you anymore. I am *done* believing anything you say to me!"

You can also do this exercise in writing, either onscreen or on paper. Make two columns, labeled *Addict Self* and *Recovery Self.* This time, instead of imagining the dialogue, write it out. Create a script between these two parts. Pay attention to what happens as you assume each identity. What differences do you experience? What happens as they speak to each other? Again, who has the power? Ask yourself the same questions noted earlier.

In early recovery, one typical dynamic is that the recovery self wants to get rid of the addict self. I have found that this never works. The addict self will always be a part of us. Clients doing this exercise invariably start out by telling the addict self to leave them alone. What do you think the addict self says in response? The answer I've heard hundreds of times is a variation on the theme "I'm not going anywhere. I'm a part of you!" This is true, but that doesn't mean you have to *obey* this part of you for the rest of your life. You don't! You always have a choice of whether you buy into the insanity caused by the addict self.

To help clients restore a healthier balance in their personality, I sometimes use a technique based on a *paradoxical intervention*. I have a client experiment with a provocative version of Step One by admitting to their addict self that they are powerless over it. It's amazing what happens next. Once a client finally admits and accepts the fact that their addict self has been running the show, they are then able to regain control over their lives. That's why this type of intervention is called paradoxical: admission of the problem of powerlessness helps us gain real power. Once clients realize that they've abdicated to this part of themselves, they're able to mobilize themselves to begin to reorganize their personality in the way Carl Jung described.

So let's return to the dialogue you are having with your addict self. Now, step back and try to describe the kind of relationship you notice between the addict self and the recovery self. Here are a few questions to help you focus on important themes:

- Which part of you felt more powerful?
- When one side asked the other side a question, did it answer or did it deflect and raise a separate issue?
- Did any compassion exist between these two parts?
- Did your recovery self ask the addict self for help?
- Did your recovery self ask your addict self what makes it want to drink and use?
- Did your recovery self ask your addict self what it can do to help?
- Did your addict self answer?
- Did your recovery self try to be there to support your addict self?

With this exercise, you're becoming aware of the quality of the interconnection between these two parts of yourself. You're striving to ease their conflict, to make them more coordinated and integrated. If these issues did not come up in the dialogue, go back and have them acted out. It could help you understand the function your addict self plays in your life, and you might find it more willing to cooperate once you take charge of it.

Summary: Building a Relationship between the Addict and Recovery Selves

The ideal relationship between your recovery self and addict self is one of coordination, with your recovery self calling the shots. This collaborative relationship will help reorganize your personality so that it will support your abstinence and recovery.

Mental health is best understood as the coordination and harmonization of *all* of the selves that populate our personality—

including the addict self, for those of us in recovery. In the words of Gestalt therapist Erving Polster, the goal of therapy is to "merge the disharmonious aspects of the person so that they [can] become joint contributors to the person's wholeness" (Polster, 2005). To recover from addiction we must learn to come to terms with our addict selves. If we try to cope with this part of us by resisting it, it will just persist and eventually control our lives. What we resist, persists.

Recovery begins with a paradox. As soon as we admit we are powerless over this part of ourselves, we begin to find ways to *live with it* without letting *it live us.* This shift in our personality reorganizes us; all the selves that make us who we are become better coordinated and harmonized as an integrated personality. The benefits of this psychic shift are far-reaching. The shift helps us recover our lost, true self and build a foundation for a new way of life based on honesty, integrity, willingness, and commitment.

Even as we embark on this new way of life, we can still experience creeping thoughts that tell us we can drink or use again with impunity. We'll address this in the next chapter.

Stupid Thing 5

Discounting the Creeping Thoughts That You Can Drink or Use Again

The addict self is tenacious: it looks for any chance to justify picking up a drink or using again. These creeping thoughts are bound to happen. Being ashamed of them, or feeling like we need to keep them a secret, will sabotage our recovery. We need to share these thoughts with someone we trust and try to understand what they mean or what they're telling us.

Clients sometimes tell me what thoughts go through their mind before a relapse. Here are some of them.

- "I'm feeling much better now. I think I can control my drinking."
- "I'm out of town—no one will know if I have a couple of drinks or smoke a joint."
- "I'm an alcoholic; I never had a problem with drugs. It should be okay if I take some Xanax."
- "I've got a terrible chest cold. Scotch in warm milk will help loosen up my chest."

- "I just celebrated twenty-five years. I think it'd be okay to have at least one glass of wine with dinner."
- "I never really liked to drink; heroin was all that really caused me problems, so it should be fine to have a couple of beers with my friends."
- "Everyone else in the NA program probably takes a drink every now and again, so why shouldn't I?"
- "I'll never let things get as bad as they were before. I know better now."
- "None of my friends seem to have a problem, so why do I?"
- "I've been clean for six months now, so I need to reward myself and go out this weekend. I'll get back on track on Monday."

It's amazing to me how often these kind of thoughts creep into our consciousness. These thoughts are common to many of us in recovery—not only newcomers, but long-timers as well. In early recovery, we are usually unprepared to deal with these kinds of thoughts. But even when we've strung together a lot of time sober, they can still knock us off balance.

One reason these thoughts bowl us over is that we think they *shouldn't* happen. This expectation is grounded in a toxic attitude: we mistakenly believe that because we received help and worked hard on our recovery, we shouldn't ever have any thoughts about getting high or drinking. This is unrealistic.

The "problem" is never the problem. Our real problems arise from our *relationship* to the experience we are having, not from the experience itself. In this case, the problem is not that thoughts about drinking or using sneak up on us. It's that we don't have the proper relationship to these thoughts. We don't know what to do about them, and they're scary.

Many of us think that having these thoughts means that something is wrong with our program—we are heading toward a relapse. The reality is that it's *how we cope with these thoughts* that will determine if we're at risk for relapse, not the thoughts themselves. So let's take a look at just what it is about our relationship with these creeping thoughts that puts us at risk for a relapse.

Shame about Having These Thoughts

The first thing that we must guard against is feeling so ashamed of these thoughts that we keep them a secret. We avoid talking about them because we hope that they will go away. This is a mistake, and it can be a deadly one! Thoughts of using are a sign of the obsessive nature of this disease and rarely go away. If we don't deal with them directly, they seem to take hold and begin an insidious process: thoughts creep into our mind that we are *not* powerless over alcohol and other mood-altering substances. And if we had any reservations about staying sober, these thoughts can amplify them.

Keeping these kinds of thoughts a secret is the worst thing you can do. The addict self thrives on secrecy and shame. So when you don't tell someone about these creeping thoughts, you are playing right into the hands of your addict self. Instead, if you share these thoughts, you reduce the risk that you will relapse.

I strongly encourage you to share these thoughts with someone you trust: your sponsor, a therapist, someone you're close to in AA or NA, a good friend, or possibly your spouse or partner. Note that if you choose to share these kinds of thoughts with a partner or someone else who is not well grounded in recovery principles, they might react with fear and anxiety. This may not be best for you or them.

So keep this in mind when you determine who you are going to ask for counsel. The person or people you pick must understand something about recovery, and they must not be overly invested in your recovery so they can respond to you from a well-grounded position.

Addiction-Related Brain Changes Play a Role

The second thing that can help us deal with these thoughts is to realize they don't necessarily mean something is wrong with our program. Thoughts of drinking or using are quite normal, and we should expect them to occur at various times during our recovery.

Indeed, these thoughts may also reflect the fact that *addiction actually changes our brains*. The current head of the National Institute on Drug Abuse, Nora D. Volkow, and her colleague George Koob have stated that the brain disease model of addiction is strongly supported by research.

> Studies have consistently delineated specific molecular and functional neuroplastic changes at the synaptic and circuitry level that are triggered by repeated drug exposure. These findings . . . are helping us understand the neurobiological processes associated with the loss of control, compulsive drug taking, inflexible behavior, and negative emotional states associated with addiction. (2015, p. 677)

I believe that this deep change in our brain is mirrored by a change in our personality. When we become an addict, we develop an addict self. Our personality changes, our thinking changes, our behavior changes, our relationships change, and our values shift in the direction that supports our addiction. We lose sight of our real self, and our addict becomes willing to do anything for the next fix—regardless of who we hurt or what we have to do.

So the fact that we're still having thoughts about drinking or using is understandable. I tell my clients that the fact that this part of you is still quite active means that you must stay in close contact with it—or else it will lead you back to drinking or using. When we break the physical bonds of addiction, we have a choice about obeying the thoughts of the addict self.

Jack Trimpey, founder of Rational Recovery, says that the "Beast"—the addict self—will always be talking to us and tempting us to drink or use. Our response to its temptations is critical to our sobriety. Here's what he suggests:

> Address it as if it were another person in this way: "You keep trying to convince me that there are good reasons for me to drink alcohol. I just want to hear one good reason why I should drink alcohol, now or in the future." Now wait for an answer. (1994, p. 161)

Trimpey goes on to say that the addict self may respond with something pathetic like "It will feel good." He claims when this happens, the addict self is on the defensive. All the addict self wants is "deep pleasure" and will go to any lengths to make us obey its command, including using warped logic.

Or the addict self may switch tactics and try to convince us that while it may not be a good idea to drink or use now, it may be a reasonable option at some time in the near future—like if we lose everything or are diagnosed with cancer or there is a nuclear war. The addict self tries to do anything it can to create a sense of conflict about sobriety. In fact, the addict self will barter our lives, our health, or even the entire human race for a chance to drink or use again. This is how cunning, baffling, and powerful the addict self has become.

Trimpey goes on to warn us not to negotiate or reason with our addict self: "Reasoning dignifies ideas of drinking, negotiation shows your willingness to compromise." He recommends that we shoot back quickly. "When you hear or feel your Beast stirring, think, *'Gotcha!'* Instead of saying 'No' say 'Never.'"

I have seen many clients use this strategy successfully. But the next suggestion can be even more effective in that it helps us get down to the causes and conditions that are making us want to drink.

Decoding the Message Hidden in These Thoughts

The third and maybe the most important way to deal with these thoughts is to understand what they are telling us. All behavior is communication, and all symptoms are directed at surviving—adopting a strategy to cope with or ease our pain or anxiety. These thoughts are communicating something about what is missing in our lives or in our recovery.

Here's what often happens when we have these thoughts in recovery. If we hit a rough spot, or if something good happens that we feel we don't deserve, we're going to feel uncomfortable or anxious, and we'll want to soothe it. In the past, we typically soothed pain or discomfort by turning to alcohol or other drugs. So now, even in recovery, thoughts of wanting to drink or use is like having a pain in our leg: the pain is telling us that something's wrong. In other words, a message is hidden in our creeping thoughts of returning to drinking or drugging.

So if part of us is trying to tell us something about what we need, *that's a positive message*. It implies that we can develop a more collaborative relationship with our addict self. If our leg hurts, it's telling us to pay attention to what's wrong. So our addict self is crying out that something is wrong—that something is hurting us and we need some help to cope with it.

This is the kind of relationship that I have cultivated with my addict self over the past forty years. I no longer view it as an enemy that I need to destroy or protect myself from. Rather, I see it as the part of me that was trying to help ensure my existence. When my addict self tells me I can drink or use again, it knows I'm in psychic distress; it's trying to help me cope with feelings of inadequacy, insecurity, grief, or some other emotional pain. When I drank, I felt whole—it filled in all the holes in my soul. It took away my insecurities, it helped me avoid my grief, and it made me feel "a part of" rather than "apart from." But it chose the wrong solution. This part of me was ignorant and misinformed, but regardless of its ignorance, my addict self was doing the only thing it knew to solve problems. Drinking was the most economical solution. But I learned in recovery that the economical solution is not always the best solution—and in this case, it's no solution at all.

That's the essence of what Carl Jung was telling Bill Wilson. Jung described the alcoholic as seeking wholeness or oneness through the use of alcohol. This meant that the alcoholic's drinking was serving a purpose, a spiritual purpose. I believe Dr. Jung captured an important aspect of what addiction is all about: it's a path we adopted to "fill in" what was missing in our development, a way to ensure our existence. Therefore this part of us—the addict self—is offering a functional solution, but one that eventually is only temporary and becomes a major part of the very problem it is trying to solve.

If I recognize that this addict self is an important part of me, then it follows that I need to learn how to connect to this part, to listen to what it's trying to tell me about what's missing in my life. It turns out that the addict self is very good at identifying those things. In this way it can help us take the next step in our emotional and spiritual development.

When I have dialogued with this part of myself, I've discovered many important things that have enriched and strengthened my recovery. For example, I realized that I hadn't addressed the pain and grief I suffered when I lost my father.

I started drinking at age twelve, shortly after my father passed away. I was in terrible pain. I didn't know how to digest this loss. My tortured self turned to alcohol to make me feel good. Consuming alcohol was a kind of a bypass operation, helping me avoid grief and pain. I soon became a teenage alcoholic. I truly believe that when I took my first drink my addict self was born. The alcohol made me feel alive and whole again. It gave me a reason to live again. You see, when I lost my father I lost the desire to live. I felt depressed. I was emptied by his loss, and the alcohol filled me back up. So instead of completely falling into the black hole that my grief and feelings of inadequacy created, alcohol helped me find a way out. True, that solution came with many side effects, but it didn't matter because I didn't know anything better at that time. It was as if I'd found a soggy life preserver that barely kept me afloat, but it was the best option available at that time.

Pathological solutions like drinking and using, which provide temporary relief to psychic pain, are actually symptoms of that very pain. These solutions have three distinct functions.

First, by soothing our distress they appear to ensure our existence. My drinking gave me reason to live when I couldn't find one within myself.

Second, they provide a clue to what is needed. Needless to say, I needed to face my grief and integrate the loss. I obviously needed help in processing this painful experience and alcohol became a temporary solution. Not once did I even think of asking anyone for help. There was reason for this, but it is still amazing to me that I had so little ability to take care of myself and respond in a healthier way to my needs.

The third symptomatic function of a dysfunctional behavior like drinking is that it's a cry for help. My drinking was like a flashing neon sign: "Berger's in trouble—help needed."

So you can see the value of unpacking what my addict self was telling me. At the time I had no clue, but today I know this to be true: my addict self has promoted my awareness of many issues in my life that required therapeutic attention.

When I have encouraged my clients to dialogue with this part of themselves, they've also discovered some very important things that were missing in their lives. Let's look at a few of them.

- Dave discovered that his addict self was telling him he needed to take more risks in his life. He had played it safe and let his fear and anxiety control him. Now Dave was sick and tired of playing it safe and wanted more out of life.
- Kennisha discovered that she was shy and awkward, and needed to develop more self-confidence and social skills. Kennisha had also let her fears run her life, and her addict self was prompting her to find some way to move beyond fear and instead honor her desire to live more fully and freely.
- Herb realized that he didn't want to face those people he disappointed. He had always felt like he was a failure to his father and to the rest of his family. He couldn't bear the pain so he drank, which eventually made him feel like even more of a failure. Herb needed to face his pain and, instead of focusing on what a failure he was to his family, to own how he was failing himself.
- Henrietta was able to see that she wanted to divorce her husband but felt too guilty to act on these feelings. Her

drinking had started late in life as a way to tolerate a loveless relationship. She hated her own passivity, her lack of courage to take appropriate action. Henrietta's addict self was telling her that she needed to face her dilemma head on and quit avoiding it.

- Jose needed to address his pain and anger. He had been molested by a priest at a very young age, which filled him with shame and other intense feelings and doubts. He often wondered what he had done wrong that God would punish him like this. But he didn't dare tell anyone; who would believe the truth about such a popular priest? So Jose swallowed his shame, rage, and insecurity; he drank. His drinking was telling him that he needed to heal this wound and face his pain.
- Sofia was a lesbian and couldn't admit it to herself. She'd been raised in a conservative household, with a father extremely critical of anyone gay or lesbian. Attracted to other girls from a very early age, Sofia denied these feelings and tried to act "normal" and date boys. But the feelings that "should" have been there, weren't. Eventually she started to drink and act on her attraction to women. Then she felt conflicted and guilty, and drank more. Clearly, her drinking was telling her she needed to come to grips with her sexual identity.

What is your own addict self trying to tell you by generating thoughts about drinking or using? Try this exercise to start finding out. Say the root of each sentence out loud, and then write down the first thing that comes to your mind. When you've completed all the sentences, repeat this procedure until you exhaust all your responses.

- My addict self is trying to tell me . . . .
- Drinking or using makes me whole by . . . .
- The issue that my addiction has helped me deal with is . . . .
- The things I don't want to face that my addiction masks are . . . .
- If my addict self spoke to me, it would say . . . .

Your answer to these prompts will help you begin to unravel what your addict self is trying to tell you through your creeping thoughts.

Summary: Congratulations—You're Normal!

I hope you can see these thoughts about drinking and using again are quite normal. They don't go away in recovery. What happens is that we learn to deal with them differently, and that's critical to long-term sobriety. We don't have to listen to them and obey their commands. We can say no or never. We can learn a new way of responding to them that honors our true self and our recovery, and helps us respond more appropriately to our needs. When we have creeping thoughts of using, we need to remember that they don't necessarily mean that something is wrong with our recovery. We need to share them with someone we trust.

These thoughts reflect addiction-related changes in our brain—and they can also give us valuable information about what's missing in our lives. It is our job to unpack the message hidden in these thoughts and get to work on learning how to better meet our needs.

Shame is often a barrier to working through these creeping thoughts. This crippling emotion comes from the idea that we shouldn't be who we are, or we shouldn't have been doing what we have done. Shame is caused by toxic attitudes that tell us that something is abnormal when in reality it is not. We need not give in to this emotion.

In the next chapter we'll explore the effects of living second-hand and blindly obeying authority. While it is important that we take direction, to do so blindly will interfere with our true growth and development. Instead, we need to learn to listen to our own best self.

Stupid Thing 6

Listening to Others When You Need to Listen to Your Own Best Self

See Stupid Thing 1—the fairy godmother syndrome. No one is right all the time, and working the Steps or any other program does not call for us to check our brains at the door—quite the opposite! Sponsors and others, even professionals, may give advice that contradicts program principles or our own intuition.

How likely are human beings to obey authority, even at the expense of their own instincts? Let's revisit a classic study conducted in the 1960s by Yale psychologist Stanley Milgram (1974). The question of obedience to authority—and its limits—was in the air because of the heinous crimes committed in World War II by Nazi soldiers following orders from their superiors. Milgram devised an experiment study to measure the limits of his subjects' obedience under increasingly challenging conditions. But to do so, he would have to find "naïve subjects" who didn't realize the true purpose of the study.

Dr. Milgram ran an ad calling for male volunteers between twenty and fifty years old to assist in conducting a Yale research experiment investigating memory and learning. But this was just a ruse. The real intention of this investigation was to determine the point at which an individual (the naïve subject) would disobey an authority figure who was urging them to act against another human being (the learner, who was actually a trained accomplice) in an increasingly severe fashion. The volunteers were compensated a modest amount for their time and transportation. Several hundred people responded to the ad, including postal clerks, high school teachers, salesmen, engineers, and blue-collar workers. Their education ranged from one who had not finished high school to those who had doctoral and other professional degrees.

The experiment was conducted in Yale's elegant Interactional Laboratory. A thirty-one-year-old male biology teacher played the role of the experimenter—the authority figure. Throughout the experiment his manner was impassive and his appearance somewhat stern. He was dressed in a gray technician's coat. Unknown to the volunteers, he had an accomplice, a forty-seven-year-old Irish-American male who people found mild mannered and likable. Unknown to the volunteer, the accomplice was trained to play the role of the learner and was really in on the whole experiment.

The experiment used the following procedures. A volunteer was assigned to show up at the Yale lab at a specific time. Another "volunteer"—actually the accomplice—showed up at the same time, so that the real volunteer thought both of them were volunteering, one to be the learner and one the teacher. The experimenter treated both of them as new volunteers.

He told them that the study was exploring whether people learn better when they are punished for making a mistake. The learning task was what we call in psychology a *word paired-associate task.* The teacher would read aloud a series of word pairs to the learner, such as blue/box, nice/day, and wild/duck. Then the teacher would read the first word of the pair, such as blue, along with four choices, such as chair, box, car, or vase. The learner was to indicate which of the four terms had originally been paired with the first word. (In this example, box is the correct answer.)

The subjects were told that the role of teacher or learner was determined by chance, but it was in fact rigged so that the naïve subject would always be assigned the role of teacher and the secretly trained accomplice would always be the learner.

The teacher was instructed to give the learner an electric shock every time he made a mistake on the learning task. Moreover—and this was the key command—the teacher was instructed to increase the shock each time the learner gave a wrong answer, and to announce the voltage level before administering it.

The teacher was then placed in front of an instrument panel that consisted of thirty lever switches set in a horizontal line. Each switch was clearly labeled with an electric voltage ranging from 15 to 450, left to right. The label also described the voltage level, from "Slight Shock" to "Danger: Extreme Intensity Shock," with the last two switches labeled "XXX." This was part of the ruse, since no electricity was actually generated by any of the lever switches.

Before the experiment, as a sample, each teacher was given an actual shock on his wrist—a shock that appeared to come from the generator. The shock was always 45 volts and was applied by pressing the third switch, thus strengthening the naïve subject's belief in the generator's authenticity.

During the test, when the teacher supposedly administered a shock, a pilot light corresponding to the switch was illuminated in bright red, an electric buzzing sound was simultaneously heard, and the needle on the voltage meter swung to the right.

It was anticipated that at some point during this procedure, the teacher would become stressed about hurting the learner and would turn to the experimenter for advice on whether he should continue to administer shocks. The teacher might even ask to bail out of the experiment.

The learner-accomplice was trained to react to the teacher's punishment by becoming more and more vocal about his discomfort and pain. If the teacher turned to the examiner and voiced his reluctance to continue with the shocks, the examiner prodded him to continue administering them as long as the learner kept making mistakes. As the voltage increased with each mistake, the learner vocally or nonverbally expressed pain, even to the point of pleading with the teacher to stop.

Intense scene, isn't it? So what do you imagine the teachers would do? When would they disobey the examiner?

Before this study was conducted, Milgram asked three groups of individuals to predict the point at which disobedience would occur, that is, at which voltage level the teachers would stop administering shocks. These three groups were a group of psychiatrists, a group of college students, and a mixed group of citizens. All of the groups predicted disobedience or defiance at some point in the experiment. The mean maximum shock level that they predicted was around 135 volts.

One more detail: the study was conducted with four variations on the proximity of the learner to the volunteer teacher. In two conditions they were physically separated, but the teacher could either hear, or hear and see, the learner's reaction to the shock. The other two conditions placed the learner right next to the teacher. In one of these conditions, the teacher actually had to hold the learner's hand down on a plate when administering the shock.

The results? In every condition, almost 50 percent (half!) of the volunteer teachers did not disobey the experimenter and continued to administer what they believed to be a very intense electric shock to the protesting subject. While closer proximity had some impact on the teachers' willingness to continue the shocks, there were still a significant number who never disobeyed the examiner—demonstrating our all-too-common tendency to defer to authority.

The study showed that when we defer to an authority figure, we sometimes mistakenly believe that they know right from wrong better than we do. (Up for debate is the significance of the fact that all of the volunteer teachers were men. But it's safe to say that in the 1960s, authority figures were even more likely to be male than they are today.) We typically defer to someone who we believe has more knowledge than we have. Sometimes it is a terrible mistake to do so.

No one was physically hurt in this study, although one could note that the study may have been psychologically harmful to the volunteer subjects. The study also showed that we have a tendency to absolve ourselves of any responsibility for our actions when we are ordered to act in a certain way, assigning ultimate responsibility to the person giving the orders. I don't believe that this rationalization is legitimate; I think that each and every one of us is individually responsible for our decisions and our actions.

The outcome of this experiment aside, I believe that personal responsibility is a crucial variable in life and in recovery. While we need to take direction and be open-minded, recovery requires us to take total responsibility for ourselves. This is a fine line to walk. It is strongly recommended that we take direction from people who have more experience or expertise than we do, such as a sponsor, clergyperson, AA or NA mentor, therapist, or medical doctor. In fact, we are told that our recovery will depend on our willingness to follow directions. We are also told, and rightly so, that it was our best thinking that got us here, that allowed us to fall into the depths of addiction. So it seems to make sense that we can't trust our own thinking. Remember, you can't solve a problem with the consciousness that created it.

There is some benefit to this advice, but I believe that it is an overgeneralization, and if applied too dogmatically, it sells us short. We are more than our addiction, or else we couldn't get well.

There are parts of us that are grounded in our own inner wisdom that we need to listen to as well. Here's where the problem comes in: *We've done such a good job desensitizing ourselves to what we really feel and believe that we've cut ourselves off from that inner voice that was telling us that what we were doing was wrong.*

We've discussed the idea that recovery is about "recovering" the missing pieces of who we are—reclaiming our lost, true self. This means that recovery is also about reclaiming our intuition. It's about coming to our senses even as we learn to live with our addict self, as described in Stupid Thing 4. We rarely do this while blindly obeying an authority figure. We need to honor the inner conflict that arises when we are given a directive that doesn't harmonize our recovery self with our true self. When some piece of advice or received wisdom doesn't sit right with our true self, we need to be like one of those experimental volunteers who said, "No, I will not administer another shock. This doesn't feel right."

When Outside Advice and Inner Voice Collide

We rightfully turn to outside guides to help us with recovery—sponsors, health professionals, clergy, and others. But their help and expertise in one area does not mean they'll provide the right guidance in another area. Learning to listen to signals from our inner wisdom is the key. I want to share with you several situations that I have seen over the past four decades in working with men and women in recovery: the stories of Brian, Herb, and Mary. Some aspects of these stories may alarm you, and in a way I hope they do. They seem outrageous because they are. Stories like these happen all the time, and they definitely help illustrate the stupid things we can do to mess up our recovery.

My intent in sharing these stories, however, is not to alarm you but to wake you up. Many great philosophers have noted that we are sleepwalking through life, thinking we are awake. And even though recovery serves as a wakeup call for many, even those of us who've been in recovery for some time will still fall asleep at times and need to wake up and come to our senses.

Brian: A mistaken sponsor

Brian was one of these sleepwalkers. Brian was what we call a "real alcoholic," which means that he only used alcohol and no other drugs. Toward the end of his drinking, Brian was consuming a quart of vodka a day. He was unemployed and unemployable for the year before he finally started recovery. His wife was disgusted with him, and his three children acted like he didn't exist. After suffering many disappointments and betrayals, they had stopped turning to him for attention years ago.

When Brian's liver began to shut down, he was admitted to the local hospital. His medical doctor had been encouraging Brian to address his alcoholism for several years to no avail. Brian didn't answer the alarm—he hit the snooze button. But this time his medical doctor arranged for a counselor to meet with Brian and his family to discuss the fact that he was dying from alcoholism.

This wasn't the first time that Brian had been confronted, but this time the result was different. Something his son Michael said penetrated Brian's resistance. As tears rolled down Michael's cheeks, he shared that the only way he could live with his father's daily drinking was to believe that his father had already died. Otherwise, it was too painful to think of his father as alive.

Brian decided to go into rehab that afternoon. He did quite well. He finally answered this alarm and started to wake up by getting honest with himself and others. But the damage he did to his family was slow to heal.

It's a sad fact that there are only a few treatment programs in the country that seriously treat the entire family, which means that they also include the children in the therapeutic process. Unfortunately, Brian was treated at one of those programs that seemed to believe that telling his wife, Elsie, that she needed to go to Al-Anon constituted "family treatment." It wasn't enough for Elsie. She and her children needed some serious help to repair the damage and heal the pain, but they didn't get it, so she and Brian were estranged. They hadn't been together physically as husband and wife for over a decade. They rarely spoke to one another and had very little meaningful contact, living parallel lives.

Elsie no longer seemed to care about their relationship. She had fallen out of love with the man she married many years ago. In fact, she said that the man she married had left their marriage when his alcoholism started.

In recovery, Brian unfortunately continued to avoid any meaningful conversation with his wife. He wouldn't dare discuss his emotions about his drinking and the effects it had on him and the family. It was just too painful, so he avoided Elsie's anger, her pain, and her contempt.

Brian had never learned how to confront conflict in a healthy way. His parents had had a very distant relationship and never fought. But he was also afraid of what he imagined Elsie would say if they authentically engaged. So he lived with dread and fear. He remained emotionally withdrawn and distant. Unfortunately, if nothing changes in your relationship other than your drinking, then nothing will change.

What Brian didn't know was that his wife was having an affair. Two years into sobriety, he inadvertently saw a text on her phone from the man she was seeing. He was devastated. He had hoped that sobriety would enable his family to heal and come back together. Many people hope that getting and staying sober will be sufficient to heal the family wounds, but it rarely is. It typically takes much more effort, just as getting sober takes effort.

After he learned of his wife's infidelity, he left the house without saying a word to her and immediately called his sponsor for advice. His sponsor was a long-timer in AA and, up to this point, had given Brian some solid advice.

But even if a sponsor can help us stay sober, it doesn't mean he or she will make a good marriage counselor. Unfortunately, this was the case with Brian's sponsor. He advised Brian to not address or confront the infidelity. He claimed that "this is a program of attraction rather than promotion, and if you continue to do the right thing Elsie will eventually let go of the other relationship and reconnect with you." Essentially his sponsor was saying that he believed that Elsie would come around after Brian logged some more time in the program, as long as he stayed sober.

Brian wasn't certain that this was sound advice. Something inside of him told him that it was wrong to take no action. This was the first time he'd differed with this sponsor, and he didn't know what to do. Brian was afraid that if he didn't address the affair he would be sending the wrong message—that he didn't care. He wanted Elsie to know that he still loved her and wanted a shot at becoming a better husband. Brian wanted a chance to save their marriage, but he didn't know what to do because he also respected his sponsor and had benefitted greatly from his direction up to this point in his recovery. He was in conflict: Did he obey his sponsor or listen to his inner voice? Brian decided to get some outside help to address his conflict.

Brian called me to set up an appointment. When I finally met Brian, we discussed the conflict he was experiencing over his sponsor's advice. Brian rightfully believed that his passivity and avoidance would just reinforce his wife's belief that he didn't really care and wasn't willing to work for the relationship. He wanted a shot at saving his marriage but didn't want to disobey his sponsor. So, for over a month, he had just accepted what his sponsor told him without speaking his mind. As Brian and I sat there talking, I noticed an interesting dynamic: Brian's problem with his sponsor was similar to his struggle with Elsie. Brian was passive; he didn't stand up to either of them. He didn't let his wife or his sponsor know what he really wanted. He played it safe and did not take a risk. This passivity and avoidance was a self-destructive pattern in Brian's life.

Here was the same dilemma faced by the men who volunteered in Dr. Milgram's obedience study. Brian's gut told him that his sponsor's advice was wrong, but he didn't want to disobey him. So he just passively accepted that advice without openly discussing his conflicted response to it.

I confronted Brian about his passivity and made him aware of the pattern I saw in his relationships. This had a very profound impact on Brian. He got angry with himself for being so passive and, as he sat in my office, he decided to call his sponsor. He told him that he deeply appreciated what he had done for him and that because his sponsor helped save his life Brian felt a deep sense of gratitude. He also wanted his sponsor to know that he was in conflict over the sponsor's advice about how to handle what was going on in his marriage. Brian asked his sponsor if he would support him if he went into marriage counseling. His sponsor said that of course he would, if that is what Brian really wanted.

Brian and his wife started marriage counseling, and for the next year they got down into the muck and struggled with years of frustration and pain. Brian and his wife finally decided to divorce, but because of all of the work they had done, they were able to have a collaborative divorce and established a truly solid friendship. The marriage counseling was tough going for Brian because he suffered from a lot of guilt and shame. But he hung in there. He grew because he didn't run away and avoid the pain. Now he is remarried and is enjoying a better relationship with his children.

The key point here is that Brian eventually honored his inner voice and struggled to reconcile it with the advice he was being given by his sponsor. It's important that we don't ignore our inner voice, that we respect it and listen to what it's trying to tell us.

We also have to be careful when we ask our sponsors to guide us outside of their scope of competence. Yes, we may trust them, but they're only human and can unintentionally send us in the wrong direction if they don't recognize and accept their own limitations. A sponsor's main role is to support and advise you in working your Twelve Step program and in how to best use your time in meetings—not to try to solve all of your problems.

Henry: Misguided medical care

Medical doctors, even when certified to practice addiction medicine, may also lack the knowledge to advise outside their skills. At least this is what Henry discovered—but it was almost too late.

Henry called me because he was anxious and concerned about the anti-anxiety medication he had been taking for the past four months. Henry had over four years of sobriety. Six months previously he'd become very anxious and believed that he was going to get in trouble with the government. He had underreported his taxes and was afraid he was going to be audited by the IRS and then sent to jail. It's important to put this in context. Henry *had* underreported his taxes, but by a total of only eight hundred dollars. Still, he acted like he had underreported millions of dollars and couldn't stop obsessing about what was going to happen to him. He imagined that he would eventually be imprisoned and then get molested or severely injured in a fight. He was doing one heck of a job torturing himself and was paralyzed with fear and anxiety.

It was at this time that he knew he needed help, so Henry called a psychiatrist who also specialized in addiction medicine, believing this doctor would have a solid understanding of both his anxiety and his addiction.

Henry met with the psychiatrist and was diagnosed with severe anxiety and panic attacks. The doctor prescribed Ativan for his anxiety and Restoral for his insomnia. Both of these drugs are highly addictive and are contraindicated for alcoholics or addicts except in extraordinary situations. When the psychiatrist recommended these medications, Henry had a fleeting thought that they might not be a good idea. The psychiatrist did inform Henry of the risks involved but played them down. Henry asked if there was an alternative treatment that would be less risky. The psychiatrist told Henry not to worry, that he would keep a close eye on him so that he didn't abuse the medication.

Four months later Henry was becoming dependent on the Ativan and Restoral, and could sense that the medications weren't working as effectively as when he first used them, which would likely mean the doctor would recommend increasing the dosage. He realized that his initial "fleeting thought" was right in the first place. He needed a non-drug alternative to treat his anxiety.

The good news is Henry caught himself before he spiraled back into his addiction. His fleeting thought was a sign that Henry was working a good program. When I explored what stopped him from listening to his inner voice in the first place, he said, "I thought the psychiatrist knew better than me. I remember what everyone told me when I was new in the program, that I needed to be open-minded and follow direction. I was torn about taking drugs, but I was in great pain."

Does this sound familiar? Does it remind you of the volunteers in Dr. Milgram's experiment, continuing to administer what they believed were increasingly painful shocks to an apparently miserable "learner" simply because an authority told them to?

Whenever we suspend our judgment or ignore our intuition that something isn't right about the advice of a professional, a trusted sponsor, or someone else in authority, we are abdicating our personal responsibility. That's exactly what Henry did, and it's also what Mary did in the following story. As you will learn, she paid a terrible price.

Mary: Deferring to a therapist

Mary had been in recovery for six years. She didn't drink, but she had a heck of a time finding emotional sobriety. Her emotional instability made it hard for her to function well in relationships. Emotionally dependent on a partner, Mary had unconsciously made many unenforceable rules about how a partner was supposed to behave to make her feel lovable and validated. If the partner didn't adhere to one of her impossible rules, she let the partner have it. Once she felt betrayed or abandoned, all bets were off.

Mary dated Trey for almost six months. They'd met in recovery, and they were very close, but once again Mary's behavior drove Trey away—but not before Mary got pregnant. Trey didn't want to be a father and said that he wouldn't be involved in the child's life if Mary decided to give birth. Mary truly wanted to be a mother, but she felt great ambivalence about having a child without a partner to help her. She also was afraid that her family and friends would look down on her. Yet underneath all that, an inner voice told her that she wanted a child, and that this was the right time for her.

Mary decided to see a therapist to help her with the decision. After three sessions Mary asked her therapist what she thought she should do. The therapist told her that it seemed like having a child under these circumstances wasn't a very good idea and might not be good for Mary's recovery. Mary decided to take the therapist's advice and have an abortion, a decision she would increasingly regret as time passed. Rather than exploring and struggling with her ambivalence on her own, Mary took the easier way, leaving it to the therapist to make this very difficult decision for her.

When Mary came to therapy with me, she wanted to work on the resentment she had toward the therapist who advised her to abort the pregnancy. As we worked through her resentment, Mary realized that she had betrayed herself by not insisting that the other side of her be heard—the part that wanted a child. When Mary accepted responsibility for her self-betrayal, her resentment toward the therapist was resolved. She integrated the lesson and accepted that she was the one who had made the decision. This realization strengthened her recovery and helped her develop a healthier relationship to the many selves that existed in her personality.

As these stories illustrate, we are often inclined to defer to authority and abdicate responsibility for our lives. When we don't honor and struggle with our ambivalence and defer instead to an authority's recommendations, we miss the opportunity to integrate the voices of our conflicting selves and create inner unity and harmony. The more emotionally and spiritually coordinated we are, the more likely we will be able to act wholeheartedly for our own mental and physical well-being.

These stories are not meant as warnings against taking advice or guidance. They are here to help you realize that your inner voice should be attended to. It is only partially true that "your best thinking got you here." That's because the "best thinking" was coming from your addict self, not your whole, true self. It was coming from your lower self, not your higher self. Deferring to an authority—be it a sponsor, medical doctor, or therapist—whose advice triggers a warning bell is a way of turning over personal responsibility to someone else. As the Milgram experiment showed, this is quite common among human beings—half of us will go ahead and administer the shock because someone else was ultimately responsible. This is unfortunate, and as you have heard, this abdication of our responsibility has the potential to damage ourselves, disrupt our recovery, and harm those we love.

To help you explore the issue of authority in your own life, finish each of these incomplete sentences with the first thought that comes to mind. Then repeat.

- My parents taught me that authority is . . . .
- I learned from my father that I should respond to authority by . . . .
- I learned from my mother that I should respond to authority by . . . .
- My own attitude toward authority has been . . . .
- The price I have paid when I let an authority figure tell me what to do, rather than listen to the voice inside of me, is . . . .
- The part of me that wants to listen to an authority figure rather than find my own resolution tells me that this is a good idea because . . . .
- I give up responsibility for my life by . . . .
- If I trusted myself more, I would . . . .
- To honor myself more, I need to . . . .

- The biggest internal conflict I have is between . . . .
- I learned not trust myself because . . . .
- If I were to honor my biggest internal conflict and take the time to resolve it, rather than look for a quick workaround, I'd have to give up the idea that I am . . . .

Summary: Learning to Listen to Our Inner Voice

There's a real dilemma when we enter the Twelve Step rooms. We are first told not to trust ourselves. "Your best thinking got you where you are at today" is often the feedback we receive as newcomers. And for the most part, accepting this concept can help us stay grounded and open-minded in early recovery. But this message can also undermine a growing sense of our true self that is worth listening to. We can also undermine our recovery if we take this point to mean that we shouldn't listen to our own common sense. After years of ignoring our inner voice, it becomes habitual to ignore it. This is a real problem because recovery is about recovering what we have lost. And, as we've seen, we have lost touch with many different parts of ourselves that didn't play well with the addict self. This means there are parts of us that are worth listening to, parts that may be wise and grounded.

We must ensure that we're letting our best selves do the thinking. How can we know? By the results! If the best of us is in charge, our life will start to click. We will thrive like never before. It's as if we're a flower that has needed to be watered, and as soon as we receive the missing nutrient, we start to blossom.

Often when we make a decision we want to know in advance that it is right. That is usually impossible. We'll drive ourselves crazy trying to predict the outcome of a decision, because the outcome is often determined by forces that are out of our control. Focusing on the outcome when we make a decision is like trying to forecast the weather. The best we can do is make a decision based on what is important and seems right for us at the time. This way, the act of making the decision—based on the values of our true self—is what makes it right, not the outcome.

When part of us is ambivalent or uncertain about a direction we are given, we need to struggle with these feelings. What does the uncertainty tell us about what is important to us? Can we reach a wholehearted decision to either follow someone else's direction or follow our own sense of what is right for us—or some combination of the two? When we feel ambivalence and internal conflict over a decision, we need to learn to deal with it rather than prematurely work around it. If we can't resolve our conflict for some reason and we decide to follow someone else's directive (as we saw in Mary's case), then we need to take responsibility for *that* choice, too.

As we live the outcomes of our choices, we will know if those choices were right for us. We need to wholeheartedly accept responsibility for deferring to someone else and use that choice as an experiment to learn from. *The main goal here is to not be a passive victim.*

I encourage you to be open to experimenting and trying on new ideas. But at the same time, to really effect change, you need to be willing to accept full responsibility for both the efforts you make and the outcomes. Keep these thoughts in mind.

- We are responsible not only for what we do, but also for what we don't do.
- We are responsible for what happens when we follow advice, and what happens when we don't.
- We are responsible for the level of consciousness and awareness that we bring to our lives and to any decision.

- We are responsible for our self-esteem, how we treat ourselves, and how we treat others.
- The bottom line is that we are responsible for our lives and for the quality of our recovery in all areas that are open to choice.

In the next chapter we'll further explore how you can empower yourself in recovery rather than be a victim. We'll focus on one specific area: prescription drugs. Going to a medical doctor to receive treatment that involves prescription drugs for certain conditions can put us on a slippery slope if we don't prepare ourselves to be assertive and protect our recovery.

Stupid Thing 7

Using Prescribed Mind-Altering Drugs When Other Remedies Are Available

Mind-altering drugs such as medical marijuana or opioids may be needed for certain conditions, but recovery requires that we use other remedies when we can. These drugs can endanger our sobriety, so we should be sure to find medical doctors who understand our disease, prescribe them only when no other treatments work, and monitor us closely.

There is an alarming trend in the recovery community: a growing number of us are relapsing after receiving medical treatment involving medications prescribed to manage pain from an injury or post-operative pain, or to treat anxiety or a sleep disorder.

It would be easy for us to blame these relapses on the doctors who prescribed these drugs. But this turns us into victims. We may be naïve or too trusting when it comes to making decisions about prescription drugs, but we aren't victims. Relapse cannot be solely blamed on the prescribers.

Of course, when there is abuse of these medications, the prescribers are culpable, too. Medical doctors have a professional responsibility to *first, do no harm.* Therefore they must go to reasonable lengths to determine if a patient in recovery from alcoholism or other drug addictions is at risk of misuse that leads to relapse when prescribed certain medications. If medical professionals don't take this step, then they clearly have a role in creating this problem. It is my hope that medical doctors will take more responsibility in their prescribing practices with members of the recovery community and get better education in these matters.

But we can't wait until medical doctors become more informed about treating people in recovery. To protect ourselves and our sobriety, we need to become more informed consumers and learn as much as we can about the mind-altering and addictive properties of the medications being prescribed for us.

It is our responsibility to protect our health and sobriety at all costs and that includes not deferring to medical doctors regarding the drugs we take. Doctors are human and make mistakes, too. So we recovering people need to know which classes of drugs are addictive and heighten our risk for relapse. We also need to be sure that our health care providers are reminded that we are in recovery and need to avoid these drugs unless they are absolutely essential. And we need to take steps to use these drugs safely when there is no alternative. (Please note that not all prescription drugs are addictive, and most are safe to use. For example, antidepressants and some antipsychotics "alter" one's mood or thoughts as they mitigate the symptoms of debilitating depression or mental illness, but they are not addictive.)

Insights from Two Experts

Given that I am not a medical doctor, I asked two colleagues, Dr. Dawn Obrecht and Dr. Harry Haroutunian, to share their insights and recommendations on this matter. I turn to them as two medical experts who are also deeply familiar with the challenges recovering people face.

We'll hear first from Dr. Dawn Obrecht, M.D., also known as DocDawn. She is a graduate of the University of Maryland School of Medicine and did an internship in general surgery and a residency in emergency medicine. DocDawn is certified by the American Board of Addiction Medicine and has been a medical director of a chemical dependency unit and a professor at the University of Colorado Health Sciences Center. Her books on recovery include *From the Edge of the Cliff* and *Who's Your Higher Power?* These books and her website (www.docdawn.com) document her own personal journey in recovery as a medical doctor, as well as stories of other people in recovery. Yes, she is one of us and has been in what she calls "successful recovery" since 1984.

DocDawn's insights and recommendations

"Based on forty years of working as a physician, the past thirty-one of which I have been in my own recovery from addiction, I have seen different ways alcoholics and addicts deal with their own illnesses and injuries.

Part of my work as clinical faculty at the University of Colorado Health Sciences Center has been teaching student and resident physicians. It is important for you to know that very few doctors receive any formal training about addiction. It is up to you to safeguard your own recovery.

Recovery from addiction is marked by profound emotional upheaval. People in recovery, especially early recovery, are usually just learning to deal with emotions. They may be happy, sad, angry, irritable, and anxious all within the course of a few minutes. Part of recovery is learning to deal with those long-denied feelings; indeed, people in recovery are learning to deal with life—life without the use of alcohol or other drugs.

Since alcoholics and addicts want immediate relief from discomfort (as well as to feel good or high as often as possible), they are likely to want all their aches and pains—whether physical or emotional or any sort of discomfort—relieved immediately. Unfortunately, many of the medications we have for these types of symptoms are mind-altering drugs, often related to the substances to which we became addicted in the first place. The excessive use of pain medications is a common cause for relapse to active addiction. Any mind-altering drug, legal or illegal, can trigger the desire to use more or to return to a previous favorite drug, including alcohol.

See if you recognize any of the flawed thought processes listed below.

- 'If a doctor prescribes it, I can take it. The doctor is the expert and must know more about addiction than I do.'
- 'My doctor knows best and won't give me anything to mess up my recovery.'
- 'It's not important to tell my doctor I am in recovery or allergic to pain medicine or tranquilizers.
- 'A script for a mind-altering drug is a free high.' (This is more honest than the first item above.)
- 'All pain, physical, emotional, or otherwise, requires a medication.' (This equals 'I deserve to be pain-free and emotionally comfortable all the time.')
- 'I'm having intense emotions. I don't want to tolerate anxiety, sadness, or insomnia. Something must be wrong with me, and it needs to be fixed with a medication.' (Note

this is not that I *cannot* sit with the feelings, but just that I don't *want* to sit with the feelings. I want to change them.)

- 'Now that I have knowledge about addiction, I will be okay and can control my use of any drug.'
- 'I don't want to tolerate aches and pains associated with normal life and minor injuries.'
- 'As long as I take it as prescribed, it's okay for a doctor to prescribe the category of drug I used to abuse.'
- 'My doctor said I'm over my alcoholism and addiction because I haven't used anything for three months.'
- 'I know that taking a prescription pain pill or anti-anxiety pill can be a slippery slope back to drinking or using, but I can handle it.'
- 'Sobriety isn't as big a deal as people make it out to be. If I relapse, I can get my sobriety back any time I choose.'

These thought processes are quite typical among people in recovery. Unfortunately, when it comes to seeking medical help, these thoughts can lead us back to active alcoholism or other drug addiction. Almost everyone in recovery has seen sober alcoholics who were in recovery for months or even years, and who then relapsed on marijuana or on a prescription sedative or narcotic. Their brains did not know the difference between alcohol and any other mind-altering drug, and upon introduction of the new drug, the brain simply said, *Cool. This feeling is familiar and I remember liking it. Give me more!* For the alcoholic or addict brain, a drug is a drug is a drug.

Since addiction is a progressive disease *whether or not we are using,* alcoholics and addicts are vulnerable even years after entering and sustaining recovery. So when a person uses a pain medication that is either an opioid such as hydrocodone or oxycodone, or a 'non-opioid-derived synthetic opioid' such as tramadol, or a tranquilizer such as Xanax or Clonidine, or some other mind-altering drug, the familiar feelings of craving are reawakened. Recovering people who have used a prescribed mind-altering medication will (if honest) tell you something like 'It lit my brain on fire.' This may be followed by 'I felt like I had to have more.'

Mind-altering prescription drugs to be wary of

"Those of us in recovery have medical problems just like everyone else. We can have an injury, chronic pain, a severe cough, anxiety, panic attacks, sleep disturbances, depression—you name it, whatever the condition is, we can get it. But just as a diabetic needs to avoid certain foods, we have to take great care with certain medications that are often prescribed for some of these conditions. And it's up to us to know about those, because the disease and our recovery belongs to us.

What kinds of prescription medications do we particularly need to be wary of? Pharmacists and medical professionals have many ways of categorizing drugs. But for our purposes, they fall into several categories: *opioid pain medications* for acute (short-term) or chronic (long-term) pain; *sedative-hypnotics,* used for anxiety and some other disorders; *medical marijuana,* used for a variety of ailments; and *stimulants,* used for attention disorders, among other issues. What follows are just some of the many drugs you need to be cautious with.

Pain medications

"Pain medications such as ibuprofen (Advil), acetaminophen (Tylenol), and aspirin are not mind-altering and don't put us at risk of relapse. However, many of the pain medications prescribed for either acute (short-term) or chronic (long-term) pain *are* mind-altering and put us at risk of relapse. Some well-known generic and brand names include fentanyl, oxycodone, Darvon, Duragesic, OxyContin, Tylenol 3, tramadol, codeine, and hydrocodone—it's a big list, and these are only a few of the more common ones. These drugs are in the *opioid* class, either derived from opium (like morphine and heroin) or synthesized to mimic the chemistry of those drugs. Opioid pain medications are extremely mind-altering, providing a rapid high, and are therefore very addictive to those who are susceptible to addiction. Non-addicts typically say, 'I don't like them. They make me stupid,' and they stop using them as soon as they can tolerate the pain.

Some statistics show that while the United States has only 4 percent of the world's population, we use over 80 percent of the world's pain pills. Please reread those numbers. We live in a society where we believe we need a pill for every discomfort. We feel entitled to be pain-free. But here are some facts about pain:

- Most pain can be adequately managed with over-the-counter, non-mind-altering medications such as acetaminophen, aspirin, or ibuprofen.
- Most pain resolves on its own in a few days or weeks.
- People in recovery can manage most pain without narcotic pain relievers. Helpful methods include ice, physical therapy, chiropractic treatment, prayer, hypnosis, meditation, and talking with others about how they managed pain.
- Especially for people in early recovery, physical pain may feel magnified because we have never dealt with it drug-free.
- Physical pain may be compounded by emotional pain. Many find that their headaches or backaches disappear

when they work the Steps, enter into psychotherapy, and deal with their emotional pain.

Some medications prescribed for cough or diarrhea also contain mind-altering opioid drugs that help suppress a cough or slow down bowel activity. These need to be avoided when possible.

Sedative-hypnotics

"Another category of dangerous drugs is sedatives. These drugs can be thought of as 'alcohol in pill form' and are all mind-altering and highly addictive. They are also called central nervous system (CNS) depressants. In addition to alcohol, the most commonly abused in this category are benzodiazepines: anti-anxiety drugs such as Xanax, Ativan, and Valium.

Maintaining your recovery requires you to stay away from prescription tranquilizers as vigilantly as you avoid alcohol. As a woman named Willie put it, 'Some days I'm just nervous. I don't use alcohol or pills to treat it. Nobody ever shook to death!' (That's an approximation—I heard her talk on an AA recording long ago.) Her point is that she has learned to live with nervous or anxious feelings. She doesn't try to make the feelings go away by using a substance; she's found other ways to deal with the problem.

If you are feeling anxious, work hard to handle it in meetings, with your sponsor, and with a psychotherapist. If you cannot deal with it, especially if your anxiety is accompanied by physical symptoms of rapid heart rate and tremors, see a physician. He or she can rule out a treatable medical condition such as hyperthyroidism or heart disease. Once you have a clean bill of physical health, you can safely use some other methods to combat the anxiety.

First and foremost, be prepared to refuse a mind-altering, addictive pill to treat anxiety. The best solution, as we'll discuss shortly, is to begin to work with a good therapist who understands addiction, recovery, and trauma. When you identify your emotional pain, you can begin to effectively deal with it. Talking and listening in meetings is crucial, too, and is part of working to resolve (or "re-solve") old trauma that you were attempting to cover up with your alcohol or other drug use. Meanwhile, until you can sit with your feelings, try meditation (see Step Eleven), exercise, and sunlight. Try going for a walk, running, or biking to help deal with the discomfort. But remember, you will still need to work through the underlying issues eventually.

Medical marijuana (cannabis)

"Now we have a new category of prescription drugs, 'medical marijuana.' Many of us docs in the field of addiction medicine believe that there's no such thing as medical marijuana because for every presumed medical use of marijuana, there is another treatment available. Marijuana is not a painkiller; it simply makes you high so you are willing to tolerate the pain. Some people find that marijuana helps them relax—but so does talking with a friend or therapist. Get my drift? There are almost no reasons for a recovering person to use marijuana. Exceptions might include treating the nausea from chemotherapy for a cancer survivor or symptoms experienced by a person with HIV. Appetite stimulation in these and other cases is another use for marijuana. Still, there are usually other medications that are effective and not as mind-altering.

Stimulants

"And then there is speed, the street name for amphetamine, one of the stimulant drugs. What's the harm in a little extra energy? Those of us recovering from abusing cocaine, methamphetamine, crystal meth, or prescription stimulants (all basically speed) are especially susceptible to relapse on any kind of uppers.

"Remember that in the strange time of early recovery, emotions are returning full force. We don't have our familiar chemicals, whatever they were, to cover or alter our moods. And our brains are still without the natural chemicals that would help us regulate our emotions better—because our brains stopped producing these chemicals, being too dependent on drugs to do this job. Typically, we are up and down, swapping happy for sad, energetic for exhausted, all within a few minutes.

Doctors not familiar with the roller coaster craziness of recovery may mistakenly diagnose other disorders that involve rapid mood swings, such as bipolar disorder or ADHD (attention deficit hyperactivity disorder). A major problem occurs when doctors attempt to 'fix' what is normal for a person in early recovery by prescribing Ritalin, Dexedrine, or Adderall, which are all stimulants—essentially speed in pill form. (These drugs are often diverted for recreational use. For example, the Adderall prescribed in this country is sometimes crushed and snorted, just like cocaine.) *None of the stimulant drugs are safe for a drug addict.* There are other treatments for ADHD, including biofeedback, mindfulness meditation, coaching, exercise, sunlight, learning to focus in small doses, and eliminating sugars, dyes, preservatives, and other artificial ingredients from the diet. Exercise is known to change neurochemistry and helps children and adults focus more effectively.

Taking care of yourself

"Finding a doctor who will support and encourage your recovery is important. If there is a doctor in your recovery community, ask him or her to either be your doctor or to recommend someone.

Sometimes a local treatment center or people in the meetings you attend can recommend someone who has helped them and seems knowledgeable about addiction and recovery.

If this is not possible, you can still find a physician sensitive to your needs. Telling your doctor you are in recovery does not mean he or she will understand; you also need to tell him or her that you cannot safely use any mind-altering drugs. If you mention to your doctor that you are anxious, be sure to say that you prefer a referral to a psychotherapist and perhaps a massage therapist rather than a prescription for a pill. If you are injured, tell the emergency room doctor you prefer to avoid narcotic pain medication if at all possible, and if you do need something that strong, you want only a few pills, not a refillable supply (or even a weeklong supply.) Ask for a referral to a physical therapist or a massage therapist. Then call your sponsor before filling the script. If your doctor is not willing to work with you and support your desire to take few or no pain pills, get another doctor!

Is it dangerous for a recovering person to use all mind-altering drugs? Absolutely. *Any mind-altering drug, legal or illegal, can trigger the desire to use more, or to return to a previous, favorite drug, including alcohol.*

While we understand and emphasize that use of any drug can be dangerous, in many cases it can be done safely. There may be times when you must use one of these risky drugs for a medical or psychiatric condition. When this is the case, take these safety precautions.

1. Let friends and family know that you are accepting a prescription for something potentially dangerous.
2. Request a very small amount of medication, perhaps one or two pills a day for three or four days, instead of,

say, eight pills a day for four weeks (or some other larger amount).

3. Afterward, bring the drugs you do not need to a pharmacist for disposal.
4. Call or visit your sponsor or others in recovery on a regularly scheduled basis (or ask them to call or visit if you miss a call) to help you keep the perspective that you are using this medicine only for severe pain and only for a few days.
5. Stay focused on recovery and getting to meetings as often as possible.
6. Use over-the-counter medications along with the prescription pain pills to make the use of fewer prescription pills possible.
7. Refuse, or use with extreme caution, any medication with these types of warnings: 'May impair ability to perform skilled or hazardous tasks' or 'May cause drug-seeking behavior. Risk increased if you have abused alcohol or drugs in the past. Take exactly as prescribed to lessen risk of addiction.'

Some case examples

"Let's turn to some case studies; they can help us learn from others what to avoid and what to do. The following are based on real cases, but the details and names have been altered to protect identities.

> Jaycee is a drug addict now in long-term recovery. When she stopped drinking alcohol and snorting cocaine, she found that she was irritable and had enor-

mous difficulty concentrating. Her therapist sent her to his supervising psychiatrist, who prescribed Adderall for her 'ADHD.' The therapist and psychiatrist did not understand that Jaycee's symptoms were consistent with early recovery. Jaycee relapsed repeatedly, each time to huge increases in her Adderall or cocaine consumption. Eventually she came to my office and we got honest about her need to be drug-free, to avoid the pills that were equivalent to cocaine. Once she stopped using 'legal speed,' she was able to stay clean.

If we are honest, some of us who have been diagnosed with ADHD or just ADD might admit that we really suffer from attention *variability* disorder. By this, I mean that there are times when we can focus and times we can't. The thing that seems to make the difference is emotions. In early recovery, it's normal to have extreme mood swings. This can be especially true as the brain is adjusting to the lack of artificial chemical input. So in this period of high emotional variability, it just makes sense that we will be unable to focus as well as when we are at our best. With time and practice, and through working a program of recovery, our emotions settle down and we learn to focus better (if not perfectly). Give yourself a chance to truly recover and work all Twelve Steps before going to a doctor because you 'can't focus.'

Gregory had been in Narcotics Anonymous and was doing very well at about three years since his last drink or drug. He was admitted to law school and began to focus closely on his studies, letting meetings and recovery slide. Gregory developed back pain and made the mistake of going to a medical doctor first rather

> than to a chiropractor, massage therapist, physical therapist, or other non-prescribing health care practitioner. He'd used narcotics, especially heroin, before he got into recovery, and now his doctor gave him a large script for oxycodone—a drug that is chemically similar to the heroin he'd been addicted to! The tragic end to the story is that Gregory relapsed on heroin. After returning to illegal drug use, he dropped out of law school and avoided the NA fellowship.

Is Gregory's story extreme, an outlier? No! The disease of addiction is extreme and extremely life-threatening. Did Gregory tell the doctor he saw that he was in recovery from addiction? Maybe. If so, he was likely met with a comment much like many of my clients heard from their former physicians: 'Oh, you haven't had a drug in three years? You are over that.' Or 'This is a prescription; it won't hurt you if you take it as prescribed.' That's just the problem! *Addicts and alcoholics cannot take any mind-altering drug 'as prescribed.'* Did you ever promise yourself you would have only one or two drinks this time? Well, it's the same with anything mind-altering.

Or maybe Gregory was not forthcoming with his doctor and did not tell him that he had a history of drug misuse. Most likely his doctor did not ask. Many doctors have told me that they don't ask because either they don't want to insult patients, have been taught not to ask, don't want to take the time, or don't know what to do with the information and feel stupid if they don't have a solution or pill to prescribe. I tell you this to emphasize that each recovering person is responsible for his or her sobriety—or clean time, if you prefer the language used in NA. Most doctors don't realize that a mind-altering drug, prescription or not, will often lead a recovering person back to active addiction.

> At about five years of recovery, Jill was scheduled for sinus surgery, an operation known to be painful for at least a week after the procedure. She lived alone, far from any of her friends in recovery, so she decided to ask a neighbor to keep her pain pills for her, giving her one or two every six hours as prescribed. She spoke to her sponsor and other recovering friends daily, and her friends picked her up for meetings as soon as she could return to them. She threw out what remained of the narcotics after five days, as she decided the pain was manageable with ibuprofen. Jill has been in ongoing recovery ever since, another fifteen years now.

Jill did things right. She used the dangerous painkilling medication only briefly, and turned control of it over to someone who could help. I have heard many versions of this story. Non-using spouses or friends can often be enlisted to keep and give out narcotics as prescribed.

> Jack is a physician. He hit bottom with his intravenous drug use as a very young doctor, got into recovery, was monitored by the medical board for several years, and returned to become an excellent practitioner. Years later, he needed a hip replacement. Jack knew his addiction had progressed during the ten or more years he had been clean, and he believed it was lying dormant, awaiting its chance to kill him. Having this belief, Jack feared relapse more than he feared a few days of pain. He told his doctors that he did not want pain medication after the surgery, and when they told him he would need it, he said, "Okay, if I need it, I'll take it, but let's wait until after surgery to decide." Jack explained

> that he knew he was not going to accept anything, but wanted to pacify his surgeon. After the operation, even during the first few days in the hospital, he used only acetaminophen and ibuprofen, declining the frequent offers for strong narcotics. He told me that if anyone asked, he would say, matter-of-factly, that on a scale of ten, his pain was an eight or a nine. He was okay with that and simply was not going to buy into the mentality that taking a dangerous drug was worth some pain relief. The pain decreased rapidly over several days, and he remains in recovery today, another twenty years later.

There are many cases similar to the ones I have just shared with you. So there is hope; you do have alternatives. To be sure, there are times when small amounts of pain medication are needed, as we saw with Jill. As with almost every rule, there *are* exceptions. People suffering from terminal cancer, HIV, neurological pain (such as RSD, reflex sympathetic dystrophy), or other disorders may need ongoing pain relief provided by one or more of the drugs I've described as dangerous for relapse. Someone on chemotherapy for cancer may find marijuana useful to treat the nausea and loss of appetite. Use of marijuana in this situation does not have to interfere with recovery. People with co-occurring disorders—mental health issues along with addiction—may require, in some cases, ongoing psychiatric care that involves drugs. But as noted earlier, most of these, while technically 'mind-altering' in that they relieve the debilitating symptoms of the disorder, are not addictive and can be used safely with supervision. The key in these cases is that the patient and doctors are all well informed about recovery—and that those of us in recovery, fellows to our suffering friend, provide ongoing emotional support rather than shame.

Finally, I'd like to share some examples of the cautious use of medication from my own history.

> During my own thirty-one years of recovery, I have had four significant surgical procedures, including a four-hour dental surgery. Each time, I used a tiny amount of narcotics and did not relapse to active addiction. After the dental surgery, on a Friday, I took one of the four low-dose Percocet pills I had accepted from my dentist on the first night. I had only the four pills, declining to fill a prescription for more. I used an ice pack, took extra strength acetaminophen (Tylenol), and sat in meetings all weekend. I was back at work on Monday. I am allergic to ibuprofen, so the only pain medication truly safe for me is acetaminophen; ice is also a pain reliever and my go-to treatment for injured tissue.
>
> A few years later, after my major abdominal surgery, my massage therapist (another woman in recovery) met me as soon as I was out of the recovery room. She worked on my back that day and the next. I again used two pain pills that first night in the hospital, then for an additional two or three days at home, returning to meetings within a few days. Since my husband is also in recovery, I had support at home.
>
> For the other surgeries, I found that acetaminophen and ice worked just fine. Of note is that when I had vocal cord surgery, I had my first and only general anesthetic. I had opted for a spinal anesthetic for my abdominal and orthopedic procedures, and local

> Novocain for dental. It is not possible to do vocal cord surgery with either of the above, so I agreed to a general anesthetic. At twenty-eight years of recovery, I was surprised when I realized that I liked the feeling of the induction of anesthesia! Since that surgery does not cause pain afterward, I did not use anything else, but I was pleasantly aware of the familiar, from very long ago, drugged sensation I got from the anesthesia.

"This last experience is a reminder: addiction is alive and well, just waiting to reclaim us at any time. Take good care!"

—Dawn Obrecht, M.D.

Words of wisdom from Harry Haroutunian, M.D.

Now let's turn to another expert. Known by all his patients as Dr. Harry, Harry L. Haroutunian, M.D., is an internationally known speaker and educator on the topics of addictive disease and its treatment. He is the author of *Being Sober* and *Not as Prescribed: Recognizing and Facing Alcohol and Drug Misuse in Older Adults*. As physician director at the Betty Ford Center, Dr. Haroutunian lectures to the patients in the various programs that include the Extended Care Program, Family Program, Licensed Professional Program, and Clinical Diagnostic Evaluation Program. He is active in the California recovering community as a recovering physician. Here's Dr. Harry's advice.

"As Dr. Dawn Obrecht noted, opioid pain medications may often have to be used after surgery, and patients in recovery have to make a very careful plan for their use with their surgeon, addictions specialist, or primary care physician. This includes limiting exposure to the medications; having a responsible, accountable family member or other loved one take charge of the medications; and avoiding risky combinations of medications taken at the same time.

Misuse of prescription medications isn't the only danger that the alcoholic or addict faces. Many over-the-counter medications are mind-altering and can also affect recovery. In particular, be concerned with Nyquil, Tylenol PM, and Advil PM. These are mind-altering and can lead to relapse. One of the most dangerous and problematic-to-assess medications misused by addicts is dextromethorphan, often found in easily accessible Robitussin DM and other cough suppressants. When taken in small doses, it can relieve a cough, but larger doses can make a person high and can create psychiatric problems that are very difficult to treat.

Dr. Obrecht has provided a helpful overview of the types of drugs a recovering person needs to be careful with. She provides useful suggestions for when and how to use these medications, as well as some alternatives to them. One further note: a very valuable medication guide can be found on the Talbott Recovery website, www.talbottcampus.com/health_medguide.php. On this site you can download an extensive list of medications that have dangerous potential for the newly recovering or long-term recovering individual. The comprehensive list can be printed out and carried with you to the doctor's office.

It is best never to make a medication decision by yourself. Those of us in recovery should discuss medications with our addiction counselor (if we have one), our family physician (if he or she is knowledgeable), our sponsor, or other knowledgeable and trustworthy resources that can assist with the decision. Most important of all, I encourage you to *inform yourself.* Never give someone else responsibility for your sobriety. It is the responsibility of the alcoholic or addict to always be on the lookout for those things that can derail recovery."

—Harry Haroutunian, M.D.

Summary: Mind and Body Are One

We tend to believe that the mind and body are two separate things. They are not. The body interacts with the mind, and the mind interacts with the body. This means that we have much more influence over our physical sensations—including pain, anxiety, and depression—than we realize.

Today, we are fortunate to have many non-drug alternatives available to treat medical and psychiatric conditions for which medical doctors often prescribe dangerous drugs. Let's review some of those options.

- Mindfulness has been found helpful in reducing stress and anxiety.
- Massage therapy has been found helpful in recovering from post-traumatic stress.
- Psychotherapy (talk therapy) has been found to be as effective as antidepressant therapy; although it appears to take longer to help, the recovery is more stable, meaning that clients who received psychotherapy relapsed less often than those who only received drug therapy.
- Movement therapy and physical therapy have been effective in reducing chronic pain and giving people tools for learning to live with it.
- Journaling can be helpful in becoming aware of what triggers pain, anxiety, or depression. Gestalt therapy and cognitive-behavioral therapy can be helpful in dealing with depression and anxiety.

So there is hope. You have many alternatives, and they're worth trying before putting your sobriety at risk.

One issue I raised earlier bears repeating. There are those in recovery who try to deceive themselves into thinking they have not relapsed when in fact they have manipulated a physician to write a script so that they can get a "free high." Addiction is cunning, baffling, and powerful.

So we must ask ourselves why we would accept a script for one of these dangerous medications without checking out an alternative form of treatment first. Moreover, we must be willing to employ some of DocDawn's and Dr. Harry's recommendations to protect ourselves. If we don't take either one of these steps, we're setting ourselves up for relapse. In fact, by taking a medication to get high rather than alleviating the pain it was prescribed to treat, we've already relapsed.

In the words of Dr. Peter Przekop, "People are not born to suffer. If you are suffering, and you are using substances to cope with your suffering, you are essentially increasing your suffering in an unimaginable fashion." Przekop is the medical director of the pain clinic at Hazelden Betty Ford Center in Rancho Mirage, California, which helps people with chronic pain who have been taking addictive opioid medications to manage it. His book *Conquer Chronic Pain: An Innovative Mind-Body Approach* has helped hundreds of people who suffer from chronic pain begin moving and enjoying life again.

In this chapter we discussed the temptation to seek a drug to solve problems such as pain, anxiety, difficulty focusing our attention, or other physical or psychic discomfort. This tendency is especially strong in the United States, and especially among addicts. DocDawn and Dr. Harry explained how this puts us at risk of taking addictive drugs again (or using them to replace alcohol), even when those drugs are legally prescribed by a doctor. Our addict self is quite creative and ingenious in the ways it can trick us into thinking that what we are doing is okay, especially if what we're doing is getting high. If you have decided you are going to relapse, then it is highly unlikely you are going to let anyone talk you out of it. But if you listen closely to yourself, there is probably a part of you that knows that this is a mistake. I hope you will listen to this part of yourself. You may have been ignoring it for too long.

Here are a few incomplete sentences to help you become aware of how prepared you are to protect yourself from a well-intentioned but poorly informed medical professional.

- When I see a medical doctor to address a medical problem, one way I can protect myself is by . . . .
- I would hesitate to assert myself with a medical doctor because . . . .
- Being responsible for my recovery in this context means . . . .
- A belief I have about the medical profession that I need to give up to protect myself is . . . .
- If I was committed to taking care of myself when I receive medical treatment, I would . . . .

In short, we are responsible for our recovery and the level of mindfulness we bring to our interaction with a medical doctor. To protect our sobriety and ourselves, we need to become informed consumers. We need to educate ourselves about medications that may be dangerous to our sobriety. And if we do need to take one of these drugs, we must take steps to ensure that we minimize the risk of relapse.

It's a fact that relapse does occur. Therefore we need to prepare ourselves to deal with this reality. Whether or not we relapse ourselves, we will inevitably find ourselves dealing with a relapse in someone we know in the program. The next chapter will help us respond to a relapse in a healthy way—rather than using shame to make a bad situation worse.

Stupid Thing 8

Shaming Yourself (or Others) for Relapse

Relapse is a common characteristic of the chronic disease of addiction. When we hide a relapse because of shame or fear of what others think—or on the other hand, when we discredit someone else who has relapsed—we set up conditions that perpetuate addiction. Seeking help for relapse is to be praised, not shamed.

A new paradigm in the treatment of addiction has emerged since the 1990s. Thanks to growing evidence from a number of addiction clinicians and researchers—including Dr. A. Thomas McLellan at the Treatment Research Institute and the late Dr. Alan Marlatt, former director of the Addictive Behaviors Institute—we now view relapse in addiction in the same light as relapse in other chronic illnesses. But this hasn't always been the case.

For too many years we viewed addiction as though it should respond to treatment like any acute illness or injury should. For example, if you broke your leg and the medical doctor set it properly, the leg would heal and you would eventually recover your ability to walk and run. Or if you had pneumonia and were treated with an antibiotic, you were expected to fully recover. Simply stated, the recovery model for addiction was based on the notion that if you completed treatment, and/or went to enough AA or NA meetings and followed directions, you shouldn't relapse; you should stay sober for life. If you did relapse, that meant you were doing something wrong, and it was your "fault." Many addiction professionals and AA and NA members alike naively applied this model to recovery from addiction because they didn't fully understand how radically addiction hijacks a person's brain.

It's well documented that only about 20 percent of those patients who receive treatment or go to AA (or other Twelve Step–based mutual help groups) remain sober for the first year of their recovery. Eighty percent experience a relapse. That means four of every five people will relapse in their first year of recovery. This data could be shocking and demoralizing for those who don't understand the typical course of treatment for a person suffering from a *chronic* illness. Medical doctors who deal with chronic illness understand that the patient will suffer many setbacks. These are not considered treatment failures; they're considered intrinsic to the nature of most chronic illnesses.

Again, my own asthma offers a good example. My asthma began in midlife when I was exposed to black mold, which triggered an asthmatic reaction. It's a chronic illness, which means that I will be living with it and will need to manage it for the rest of my life.

When I first manifested breathing problems, my medical doctor attributed them to exercise-induced asthma, because at that time the symptoms only appeared during or after exercise. My medical doctor, an internist, treated my symptoms accordingly and provided me with an inhaler. He misdiagnosed the problem, and within a month I was hospitalized because I could barely breathe.

During my hospitalization I was treated with the standard asthmatic protocol and received several nebulizer treatments with various drugs. None of these worked. My breathing did not improve. I did not respond to the typical means of treating a severe asthma attack. When the attending doctor decided to treat me with a very strong antibiotic, I started to recover. Instead of continuing care with my internist, I was referred to a pulmonologist who started me on steroids, Advair, and an inhaler, in addition to several courses of antibiotics. Still, it took almost two years to get my asthma under control. I had several relapses that required stepping up my efforts to address my symptoms. Today I manage my asthma with much less effort, but it initially took a massive effort to get me to breathe normally.

No one tried to shame me for my multiple setbacks during those two years. It takes time to work out the correct protocol for an asthma patient, and each patient is different. And with so many medications, it's easy to miss a dose, or take too much, or forget to renew a prescription—just like it's easy to slip up in our addiction recovery plan and relapse. It is *hard* to change life patterns, and moreover, none of us wants to feel like we can't be "normal" and live like everyone else. That kind of mental resistance is typical of any chronic illness that requires management. Sound familiar?

I hope this analogy makes sense to you, because we alcoholics and addicts need to cultivate the same attitude toward our problem and ourselves that I and other chronic disease sufferers do.

So this brings us to the question, What is our best possible attitude toward a relapse?

Toxic Attitudes That Prevent Us from Learning from a Relapse

To answer the question I just raised, let's first discuss some common toxic attitudes or responses to a relapse. In my experience, five faulty assumptions are among the most common myths that alcoholics and addicts tend to believe about relapse—perhaps without realizing it.

- *A relapse always means that I don't want to get sober.* This is utter nonsense. Most of my clients who relapse sincerely want to stop drinking or using. So a relapse does not mean that they aren't motivated to get sober or stay sober. It means they simply don't know how—often because they are either ignorant of or desensitized to their needs at their particular stage of recovery. In chapter 1 we discussed the need to develop the facility of inward searching—searching within ourselves to discern the best path for us—so that we can learn from our experience. A relapse contains important information about what is needed in your recovery—and what is missing. Analyzing a relapse and understanding its message is crucial to getting back on track and staying sober. I'll provide you with a few tips on "unpacking" a relapse later in this chapter.
- *A relapse means that I'm not working a good program.* While it may be true that certain areas in your recovery may need to be tightened up or addressed, a relapse doesn't mean that the program you were working was "bad," any more than concluding that my first asthma medications (which did not work for me) were bad. This is an overgeneralization—a form of black and white thinking that is toxic to recovery and creates many problems in itself. A relapse is saying that something else is needed; it doesn't necessarily mean you were or are working a completely deficient program. In fact, if you relapse and reach out for help, you are working a great program.

- *A relapse means that I'm starting all over again—that I'm a newcomer.* This is another example of the black and white thinking that is a hallmark of toxic beliefs. The reality is that can't erase what you've learned in recovery prior to your relapse. Regardless of the nature of your relapse, you still possess the knowledge and insights you accumulated from the work you've done in your recovery. The recovery tradition of counting "sobriety" as our latest number of uninterrupted days without alcohol or other mood-altering drugs troubles me a little. This makes it seem like we have to go back to home base and begin again every time we relapse. If I counted my asthma-free days that way, I'd be totally depressed! Sometimes I wonder if we need a different way of keeping track of sober time, a system more in line with what it means to recover from a chronic illness.
- *To prevent another relapse I should be critical of and punish myself.* Berating yourself or shaming yourself for a relapse will not help you learn from the experience. This is one of those futile self-improvement games where you come off as always wrong, inadequate, or incapable so that no one expects anything of you. (More on this topic in my earlier book *12 Stupid Things That Mess Up Recovery.*) In fact, you are likely to relapse again if you play this game with yourself. Why? Because beating yourself up undermines the learning process. It's an established fact that we learn better through rewards and praise than with punishment. Self-contempt doesn't prevent a relapse; it is more likely to ensure one. We suffer from a chronic illness that requires ongoing care and management.

This requires that we cultivate an attitude of compassion based on self-concern, self-respect, and self-support.

- *I should be ashamed of myself for relapsing.* Shame is a common response to a relapse and often causes us to lie about what has happened. We go underground and withhold the truth from our sponsor, from our peers in AA meetings, from our spouse or family, from our best friends, and even from our therapist. We feel horrible about falling short of our goal and letting our loved ones or friends down. Shame is based on the toxic belief *I am a mistake.* Unfortunately, a relapse may seem to validate this sense that we are losers. Shame must be neutralized if we are going to integrate the lessons inherent in a relapse.

One easy way to identify a toxic attitude or belief is that a *should* is always embedded in the concept. *Shoulds* wipe us out; they sabotage recovery because they're disconnected from reality. They are foreign ideas that are not born from our own experience and wisdom; they're *someone's else* idea of who or what we are supposed to be. They're often ideas that we have swallowed whole from the authorities in our lives and have dedicated our life to actualize. This is why members of AA are encouraged to let go of their old ideas, or the result will be nil.

The psychological mechanism operating here is *introjection,* which refers to the unconscious adoption of other people's ideas or beliefs. A *should* is an introjected concept—a concept that we've internalized to please our parents, to fit in with our peers, or to live up to cultural expectations.

Here's an analogy: adopting an introjection is like swallowing a walnut whole, without breaking the shell. The walnut cannot be digested because it's encased in this hard shell. If we broke the walnut open, then we might be able to digest the meat inside. Or we might discover that the meat is rotten and won't be nutritious. We need to break all these "walnut *shoulds*" open to see if they possess something of value to ourselves.

Because we are driven to belong, to feel accepted and to be loved, we often go to any lengths to achieve emotional and existential security. We lose our true self and dedicate our lives to becoming someone we think we should be—someone else's idea of the ideal person, rather than the true self that emerges from our core.

Any belief, attitude, or behavior that acts against the realization of our true self is toxic and therefore destructive to our recovery. On the other hand, a belief, attitude, or behavior that supports the realization of our true self and potential will nurture our recovery self and our well-being. So let's now turn our attention to beliefs, attitudes, and behaviors that are useful when we relapse.

Nourishing Attitudes That Help Us Learn from Relapse

All nourishing attitudes and beliefs we may hold about a relapse are grounded in accepting that we suffer from a chronic illness and therefore haven't failed. We pick ourselves up, learn from our experience, get back on track, and stay sober. So let's look at some of the attitudes and beliefs I encourage my clients to experiment with to see if they help them understand their relapse and develop a more solid program of recovery. You might want to consider these ideas yourself when you are confronted with your own relapse or the relapse of someone you care about.

- *A relapse means that I need to be more supportive of myself and my needs in recovery.* A relapse tells us something is missing in the way we are coping with a problem, a feeling, or some other issue that is causing us anxiety or concern.

Therefore we need to do something different. Often we need to learn to soothe ourselves instead of turning to alcohol and other drugs to regulate our emotional discomfort. Self-soothing is one of the core skills needed for emotional sobriety. The earlier we focus on emotional sobriety in our recovery journey, the more likely we are to reap its benefits and see it as essential for our long-term well-being. (More on emotional sobriety in my book *12 Smart Things to Do When the Booze and Drugs Are Gone.*)

- *Why I relapsed isn't as important as what I do about it.* Focusing on the solution is more important than getting lost in the whys. Too often, *why* questions send us off looking for someone to blame (which is irrelevant and focuses our energy on the wrong issue), or they point us toward fruitless intellectual searches. When we see relapse as an opportunity to change, we begin to empower ourselves to take responsibility for our choices and come to grips with who we are and what we need. This is what taking responsibility is really about: response-ability, the ability to respond. For example, many of us drink and use partially out of social anxiety, to ease debilitating fears about who we are. If we are unable to find satisfying ways to meet our needs for belonging and acceptance, then we will continue to turn to alcohol and other drugs (or other external solution) to solve a problem that only we can solve.
- *I may have made a mistake, but I am not "a mistake."* Though in my personal life I am not a religious person, I love the line from a song that says "God don't make no junk." If only I could have internalized this attitude

early in my life, I'd have been better able to forgive myself for my wrongs and accept the love and support that were available to me. The culprit here is shame, the internalized sense that "I am a mistake." And shame comes from internalizing an idealized notion of who we should be. How do we come to grips with the power of this notion and get free of this shame? One way is to make the claim explicit. For example, in dealing with my own idealized notion, I had to declare out loud, "I must do everything perfectly," because that's exactly what my idealized self believes. Oddly, once I said it, I could hear just how foolish the belief was. This declaration started to set me free. This simple action is related to the *paradoxical theory of change* discussed earlier. We change when we own what we are doing. For example, when we quit pretending that we are in control of alcohol and admit that we are powerless, paradoxically, we begin to reclaim our personal power. Similarly, when we quit pretending we're honest and admit that we lie to suit our wishes, then, paradoxically, we are free to become more honest. We will continue to feel like a "mistake" until we admit our crazy, unrealistic expectation to be perfect. That's because if you have no room to make a mistake, you'll end up feeling like a mistake every time you make one.

- *My relapse doesn't define me, but what I do about it does.* We are much more than our behavior suggests at any point in time. How we respond to our relapse defines us much more than the relapse itself. Remember, the "problem" is never the problem; the *real* problem is

> how we're dealing with it. The quality of our sobriety is determined by how we interpret and respond to our experience, not by the experience itself. In fact this attitude—that our response to a situation is the most important factor—is the hallmark of emotional sobriety.

As you can see from the theme of these nourishing attitudes, they are based on authenticity and accepting reality as it is.

Shame has come up several times in our discussions of both toxic and nourishing attitudes. In my decades of helping people deal with addiction and recovery, time and again I have seen shame sabotage great progress. So let's turn our attention to a brief discussion of shame, and then I will provide you with a few suggestions to help you unpack a relapse.

Addressing shame

You must address shame if you are going to get and stay sober. Even if you are unaware of feeling shame, it is likely to be an undercurrent in your life—a powerful, hidden undertow that can pull you under if you aren't prepared for it. Many people who are struggling to get and stay sober are suffering from toxic shame. You see, a part of us has to feel worthy of recovery to take the necessary steps to get sober and stay sober. If we don't feel worthy of recovery, we will sabotage it.

This definition of shame reactions comes from Gary Yontef, a therapist, author, professor, and cofounder of the Pacific Gestalt Institute training program. He describes them as

> . . . negative emotional and evaluative reactions to oneself, to what one is, how one is, what one does. . . . For the shame-ridden person, exposure, especially as inadequate or bad, brings up an intense affective energy that is almost intolerable. (1993, p. 490)

Shame is born of self-contempt and self-hate. Early in our lives many of us rejected who we really were to become what we thought we should be: the idealized self, the glorified self that we believed would solve all our problems. Well, it didn't. Our idealized self created a whole new set of problems, including self-hate for never measuring up. Famed psychoanalyst Karen Horney, who challenged some of Freud's beliefs, described the problem like this:

> The glorified self becomes not only a *phantom* to be pursued; it also becomes a measuring rod with which to measure [our] actual being. (1991, p. 110)

So we inevitably fall short of the unrealistic goal of becoming someone we are not, of becoming perfect.

Self-hate reveals the rift in our personality that started with our creation of an idealized self that supersedes our true self. We experience this split or fragmentation of our personality as a civil war in which our true self is at war with our idealized self. And as with any war there are many casualties, the most prominent being our spontaneity and our ability to sincerely act on our own behalf. We became lost to a tyranny of "shoulds," self-hate, and unenforceable rules. We imposed a ridiculous set of demands on ourselves and how we should feel, think, and respond. We mistakenly believed many ludicrous things: that we should be above being bothered by anyone or what they do to us, that we should sacrifice everything for approval, that nothing should control us, and that we should be able to make someone love us. The underlying idea is that we should be in complete control of ourselves with no limitations. That's because the idealized self is a sort of "superbeing," always in control, always able to be pleasing to others (and worthy of love), never making a mistake.

This helps us understand the difficulty so many people have in admitting and accepting that they have a chronic illness. How could a superbeing have an illness, especially one like addiction where relapse is possible, where it has to admit its powerlessness? Our shame controls us, which suggests what we need to do to shed this yoke.

To move beyond shame, we need to take these steps.

- We need to increase our awareness of the dynamics of shame and the fact that we have a choice over how much power we give it.
- We need to free ourselves from the automatic and excessive self-attacking that characterizes shame.
- We need to cultivate compassion toward ourselves and our problem.
- We need to replace shame with a sense of authentic guilt over the real wrongs we've done—a sense that is guided by our own values, not governed by our "shoulds."

As you read this, you may find yourself saying, "What an order. I can't do it!" Do not be dismayed. No one among us can pull this off without a substantial amount of help and effort. The inward searching I mentioned earlier will help facilitate this process. It will help you become aware of yourself and others, it will help guide your action, and you will trust that growth emerges from tolerating discomfort.

Unpacking the lesson in a relapse

How do we address a relapse? Here is some practical advice. First, get completely honest with someone about what's been happening in your recovery. You'll have to start by owning that it is difficult for you to be honest about your drinking or using. Try to find all the words that reflect your true feelings about being honest and what made it okay for you to be dishonest. This is an important step in regaining your integrity.

The next step is to discover and uncover what has been missing in your recovery. Once again, transparency is essential. Use the following list of incomplete sentences to help you identify what is missing:

- The hardest thing about staying sober is . . . .
- The part of me that sabotages my recovery convinces me . . . .
- I justified drinking or using by telling myself . . . .
- I imagine that a life free from alcohol and other drugs would be . . . .
- Sobriety means . . . .
- My addiction prevents me from . . . .
- If I were more honest with myself about my drinking or using, I would realize . . . .
- What I secretly despise about recovery is . . . .
- If the part of me that wants to stay sober could speak, it would say . . . .

Please share your responses with someone who can help you analyze what you are discovering and integrate it into your recovery self.

Summary: Listening to Relapse

If a patient is being treated for hypertension, the physician may try several medications before finding the one best suited for the patient. Hypertension patients typically fall back into behaviors that contribute to their condition—sedentary habits, high-salt diet, and so on—so they have to get back on track and have their medication adjusted as they keep working on the lifestyle changes.

It's the same for the chronic disease of addiction. If you relapse, you have to "unpack" what your relapse is saying about what you need to stabilize your recovery. It may take some time for you to figure out how to interpret your relapse and respond to it in a way that helps you move forward.

It is also essential to challenge any toxic attitudes that prevent you from facing and learning from a relapse. These attitudes create shame and other toxic emotions that undermine your recovery.

Instead of letting toxic attitudes rule your life, cultivate nurturing attitudes. Use the following concepts to guide your response to a relapse:

- Relapse means that I need to be more supportive of myself and my needs in recovery.
- Why I relapsed isn't as important as what I do about it.
- I may have made a mistake, but I am not "a mistake."

My relapse doesn't define me, but what I do about it does. I hope these ideas help you learn from a relapse and prevent future ones.

As we've discovered, toxic attitudes make it difficult to support ourselves and our recovery. In the next chapter we'll explore more of these sabotaging attitudes so we can overcome them in our recovery journey.

Stupid Thing 9

Clinging to Toxic Attitudes That Sabotage Recovery

We need to strive to replace toxic attitudes and beliefs with ones that will add to who we are, that are nourishing and nurturing to our recovery.

We've seen how toxic attitudes can create a deadly and insidious process that undermines our ability to realize our potential. They interfere with our development by supporting the growth of the false self, rather than the real or authentic self. They falsely instruct us to pursue goals that are unattainable and unrealistic. Often these toxic attitudes are based on cultural myths that we believe are true until something happens to cause us to question their validity.

For example, the idea that desire equals ability is a toxic attitude. Our culture emphasizes the notion that we can do anything as long as we set our mind to it. This myth tells us that if you have enough desire it will magically create that ability. Now an important thing to keep in mind is that toxic myths often possess a partial truth. While it's true that desire can motivate you to develop a particular ability, the reality is that it takes more than desire. It takes effort, natural talent, good instruction, a certain attitude toward learning, and many other crucial variables. Desire is not enough. It's an important ingredient but not a sufficient ingredient.

And that delusion can hamper our enjoyment of life. For example, I love tennis and play it whenever I get a chance. Over the past three decades I've developed some decent abilities on the court, but I guarantee you that I will *not* be playing in the final or even the first round of the US Open next year. My desire is strong enough, but my serve, forehand, and backhand just aren't good enough. If I believe that desire is all I need, then when I realize that I'll never reach that level, I could easily give up and not enjoy playing tennis any more.

I believe this delusion kills countless well-intentioned plans. We want immediate results, we want to instantaneously master things, and we don't want to put in the hard work and practice to develop the skills that we actually do have. In fact, Dr. Harry Tiebout observed this about alcoholics in particular (1999). He noted that certain infantile characteristics persist into the adulthood of the alcoholic, such as wanting to do things in a hurry and wanting immediate results. He was observing that we need to challenge our immature beliefs and grow up.

I couldn't agree more. Becoming aware of our toxic attitudes and replacing them with nourishing attitudes is crucial to getting and staying sober. Let's first review the differences between toxic attitudes and nourishing attitudes, and then we will explore several toxic attitudes that sabotage recovery.

The Difference between Toxic and Nourishing Attitudes

Toxic attitudes are an outgrowth of the false self. We become tyrannized by these attitudes, which dictate how we *should* feel or act. We can recognize them because they always contain ridiculous and unattainable standards by which we measure our behavior. You know the ideas I mean: I must always look or feel great; I should never make a mistake, especially in public; I must be the best at everything—I am not worthy of love unless I reach an ideal weight, earn more money, run in the right circles, and so on. These standards make it impossible to develop any true self-esteem, or a cohesive and solid sense of who we are.

These attitudes are based on concepts we have swallowed whole without critically examining their validity or relevance for our lives. We don't digest or integrate these attitudes into our personality because they're like foreign bodies. Remember, embracing toxic attitudes is like swallowing walnuts whole without removing the shell. Nevertheless, these attitudes drive our behavior so that we play a false role counter to our true self. It can feel like these *shoulds* are running our lives as our true self passively stands by.

Toxic attitudes interfere with our freedom to experience ourselves, our world, and our recovery *in our own way*. They cultivate fear, shame, and alienation from others, and create a fragmented, rigid self that is unable to cope with life on life's terms. On the other hand, nourishing attitudes foster freedom, a passion for living, heightened awareness, authenticity, and acceptance of our individuality and that of others (Greenwald, 1977). They encourage us to embrace our uniqueness rather than demand conformity to some external standard.

Nourishing attitudes create emotional sobriety and encourage the growth of our true self. They stimulate feelings of joy, centeredness, contentment, serenity, flexibility, and creativity. They foster the development of a strong, cohesive self that can cope with disappointments *and* success and can keep our unhealthy demands in check. They generate the resilience and humility that can help us maintain our emotional balance and take responsibility for our feelings, actions, beliefs, and choices, all of which are the building blocks of self-esteem.

Sheila's story

Sheila is a very bright woman who recently celebrated two years of recovery. A high-level paralegal with an excellent reputation, she moved up the ranks of her law firm by consistently performing above expectations.

The problem is that Sheila thinks that she has everyone fooled. She believes that she is not really that bright or knowledgeable. She has very little insight into how harshly she judges herself. She believes her attitude toward herself is grounded in reality, when in fact it is based on a toxic attitude. She knows many areas of the law well, but because there are a few areas she's unfamiliar with, she feels stupid.

Her boss sometimes teases her about the gaps in her knowledge; for example, she feels humiliated when he asks her a question about torts that she can't answer. She's so afraid he'll ask her one of these perplexing questions that she goes out of her way to avoid him—despite her success and position in the company.

When I asked Sheila what would make her feel smart, she instantly replied that she should know all the areas of the law that she works in. The attorney she works for seems to know these things, so why shouldn't she know them? The fact that she didn't go to law school is irrelevant, as far as she is concerned.

The essence of her problem is a toxic attitude that bases her self-esteem on the unrealistic expectation that she know everything that everybody else knows. When she doesn't, Sheila becomes an emotional basket case. Her drinking used to help her deal with these feelings, but now that she is sober she acutely feels the pain and frustration of not meeting these impossible standards.

Sheila is trapped by this toxic attitude, and she doesn't even realize it. She believes her boss is sadistic and teases her because he knows that she is going to feel humiliated. There may be some truth to that, but if she could get rid of the toxic myth of needing to be perfect and replace it with a more nourishing attitude that recognizes her true worth as she is, he wouldn't be able to push her buttons. She could see that the problem lies with him, not her.

Attitudes That Undermine Recovery

Let's explore some of the most common toxic attitudes that can sabotage recovery.

"We are selfish and inconsiderate when we put our own needs ahead of others."

This toxic attitude is actually taught by some Twelve Step adherents because of a basic confusion about the concepts of selfishness, self-centeredness, ego, and self. *Self* is often confused with *ego,* and we in the Twelve Step rooms know how dangerous our egos can be. Ego is equated with being self-centered and selfish, and we know that self-centeredness helps fuel our addiction.

But it's important that we draw a distinction between our *lower self* and our *higher self* when we speak of self-centeredness. Our lower self is driven by selfishness and greed; it is only concerned with getting what it wants. Our lower self is our addict self; it is manipulative, seeks glory, and is focused on *having* rather than *being.* Its motto is, "If one is good, more will be better." The ego that Bill Wilson warns us about is actually our lower or addict self. This lack of distinction between the lower and higher self in the Twelve Step rooms is evident in the common misinterpretation of AA as a "selfish program." One of the main goals of working a Twelve Step program is to reduce our self-centeredness, the inflated ego of our addict self.

The program is selfish only in that staying sober must be our highest priority.

I think the confusion stems in part from the many meanings that the word *selfish* carries. That's why I prefer the term *self-concerned.* In fact I believe that we become selfish when we don't know how to take care of ourselves. Self-concern does not adversely affect our ability to love others or our willingness to be of service to them. In fact, we can give more authentically if we're in touch with our capacity to give to others and still take care of ourselves. We cannot give something that we don't have. And if we aren't concerned for ourselves and don't take care of our own recovery, we won't be much good to anyone.

If we can stay grounded in our higher, spiritual self, then it will be our recovery self that speaks and acts.

"All I need to stay sober is AA" (or NA, SMART Recovery, you name it). This toxic attitude prevents us from finding the full benefits of sobriety and personal growth. AA and other programs can be essential to dealing with our drinking or using, but it would be naive and limiting to think that they're all we need. As we learned in our discussion of Stupid Thing 3, "Confusing Meeting Attendance with Working a Program," *passive dependence on any idea that limits our possibilities for emotional growth is dangerous to our recovery.*

I talked earlier about the trauma of losing my father at age eleven, when I was too young to have many effective coping mechanisms. Instead of facing the loss and pain, I coped with them by trying to stop needing anything or anyone. I froze up inside.

It wasn't until I joined an encounter group at the age of nineteen, early in recovery, that I discovered the capacity to deal with this loss and trauma. In the spirit of the times, the group leader, Sasha, was a hippie anthropologist turned humanistic psychologist who had long blond hair, wire-framed specs, Birkenstock sandals, shorts, and a colorful Hawaiian shirt. Sasha opened up the weekend encounter group by instructing us to close our eyes and search our feelings to see if there was someone we needed to say goodbye to, someone we had not completed grieving about. When I closed my eyes, my father immediately came to mind.

When I shared this with the group, Sasha tossed a pillow in front of me and told me to say goodbye to my father now. Wow! Immediately the dam that blocked me from feeling my grief broke wide open. Over the next four hours I sobbed, I screamed, and I raged. I yelled at God, my father, my mother, and my grandfather for betraying me. I grieved and suffered a deep, gut-wrenching pain. I remember wondering if I was going to crack under the sheer weight of these feelings, but eventually I experienced feelings of acceptance, peace of mind, and calmness of heart. This result caught me by surprise. My father was gone, but I found myself that night. I felt alive for the first time in many years—and without the use of drugs. Many people in recovery have experienced such a breakthrough when they allowed themselves the opportunity to resolve ("re-solve") a trauma.

This experience helped me solidify my foundation in recovery. It showed me a more effective and healthier way to cope with my pain, grief, and loss. Without that encounter group, I might have had a breakthrough experience later in AA, but perhaps not such a profound one.

So if you ever find yourself saying that all you need is this program, or that therapist, system, or whatever, beware: this toxic attitude can limit you from other experiences that could possibly help you in unimaginable ways. Be open-minded and experiment—especially if you are stuck and the program you have been working doesn't seem to be helping you get a better handle on your recovery.

"I just want to be happy: happiness is what life is all about."
This toxic attitude seems to be shared by pretty much everyone in the United States, but it's especially common among people in recovery. We can buy into the unrealistic belief that we should always feel good and be happy.

Many people come to see me because something is missing in their lives. They have a sense there should be more to their recovery, and they seek my services to see if I can help them discover new possibilities. When I ask them about their goals for therapy, a common response is "I want to be happy." They tell me that they have been working their recovery program for some time, and they wonder why they're still struggling with their fears or anxieties or depression or marriage (or whatever), and aren't still completely happy.

My response often surprises them. I tell them I'm not interested in helping them become happy. Rather, I want to help them become more *alive*. Being alive means experiencing wide-ranging feelings. These can include happiness, but if we're fully aware, we will also feel sad, insecure, inadequate, confused, and angry as well as confident, joyous, compassionate, excited, and myriad other human emotions.

Why do I prefer to help people be alive to their feelings rather than just being happy? When we were using, we desensitized ourselves to our feelings and experiences. We were often trying to be "happy" as a way to alleviate whatever pain existed from our past or in the present. We tried to live in only one predetermined dimension and feared experiencing all the dimensions of our humanity.

The toxic attitude that life is only about being happy prevents us from learning how to face the demands that life sets before us. It also mutes the joy of living. If we learn how to face life on life's terms, we will feel the genuine happiness and contentment that come as a result of being fully open to all our experiences, including our depression, disappointment, or sadness. The day has meaning because there is a night. We need to fully experience all that we are to feel true happiness. Moreover, a life spent only seeking happiness is often a life spent avoiding risks and opportunities for growth. This mindset is fueled by our fear that we can't cope with the pain or challenges a new discovery about ourselves might cause.

"I am incapable of dealing with my mistakes, shame, or other emotional pain."

This may be the most limiting and insidious of all toxic attitudes. We believe ourselves too fragile to cope with our painful or shameful feelings. This position minimizes our true potential—and it is rampant in our society. We become pain-phobic. We develop all kinds of ways to avoid our pain or to avoid any experience that might indicate that we're not the self we believe we should be. You can see how this goes hand-in-glove with the toxic attitude that we must be happy, since dealing with shame, mistakes, and other pain is going to be uncomfortable.

Avoidance is the name of the game, and we learn to play it all too well. And when we can't come up with a psychological maneuver to avoid our pain, we turn to drugs or other addictive behaviors to avoid our emptiness, loneliness, or feelings of inadequacy.

Our avoidance reveals that we believe we are incapable of handling our pain. I made a career out of avoiding my feelings, such as the pain of losing my father. My father's death seemed unbearable, but once I had the support I needed from a very good therapist and a fine AA sponsor, I allowed myself to feel the tremendous pain that I'd been avoiding since his death. This reconnected me to myself because when I ran away from my pain I ran away from myself. When I faced my pain, I found myself.

Forty years of clinical practice have shown me that we are much more capable then we realize. We have the potential to grieve, cry, suffer unbelievable losses, rage, or trauma—and also to forgive, both ourselves and the people we think caused the pain. We can integrate the most horrendous experience and grow from it. This is a remarkable capability that most of us are born with.

When we get out of our own way, we discover an organic wisdom that propels us to complete whatever is incomplete. This psychological imperative flows freely when we are operating from our true self. When we get in the way of flowing with our experience, it's because we believe we shouldn't be feeling what we're feeling or that we can't cope with the feelings that are surfacing. These beliefs are what undermine our very ability to cope.

If you are aware of some pain you are avoiding, and sense that it's too big to deal with by yourself, seek out the services of a good therapist and see if he or she can give you the support you need to finish your unfinished business. Don't let the toxic attitude that you can't handle the pain prevent you from fully experiencing your life.

"I shouldn't have any stress if I want to stay sober."

We've all heard time and again about how bad stress is for everyone, so it's understandable that we develop the attitude that staying sober means getting rid of all the stress in our lives. There's even been research that indicates that stress is one of the main reasons people drink or use.

It's true that reducing our stress can help us stay sober, but unfortunately this is often misinterpreted as sheltering ourselves from life. Like the toxic attitude that we must be happy, we're saying to ourselves that we shouldn't feel any discomfort. But stress is a part of life, and rather than trying to eliminate it, we need to learn how to better cope with it and learn from it. Even positive experiences can create stress. What makes stress a problem is the meaning we assign to it and how we deal with it.

If we feel that there is something wrong with us simply because we feel stressed, we're going to make ourselves more stressed and less capable of coping with it. Instead of putting ourselves down and seeing stress—or any emotional discomfort—as a threat, we can see it as a signal that we need to pay attention to a part of our lives and recovery that we've been neglecting. We can trust in our ability to identify and deal with the situation. When we improve our ability to view stress as a natural occurrence, we are better able to bring all our recovery resources to cope with it.

Unhappiness and other emotional pain, stress, doldrums in our recovery program, indecisiveness, and any number of other negative states are natural occurrences; they're a part of life. A core concept of emotional sobriety is that life is what it is, and it's how we cope with life that matters. Remember, the problem is never the problem. The problem is better understood by looking at how we are reacting to the situation at hand. In fact, I define emotional sobriety as *the state of mind that exists when what we do becomes the determining factor in how we feel.* Emotional sobriety is about keeping our emotional center of gravity firmly anchored within us.

"Marriage or relationship trouble always means that something is wrong with my recovery."

This toxic attitude is another variation on the theme that we always need to be happy. It is commonly held by people in recovery and often shared by their partners, whether they are also in recovery or not.

Relationships naturally involve conflict. If you and your partner embrace conflict and dig into what it means, you will find that your trouble is likely caused by something that is unrealized and unfulfilled in your emotional life. In other words, the trouble relates to your level of emotional sobriety or maturity. It shows you what is missing; it highlights areas of your personality that need to be developed, reprioritized, or strengthened to create a healthier relationship. Remember, this is the focus of Stage II recovery.

I call this process *grinding.* As a stone is ground by sand and water, its rough edges smooth out and it begins to glow. In the same way, grinding refines and polishes us (Berger, 2006). It helps us realize our true potential as a partner and as a person.

Among recovering people who are married or in a committed relationship, troubles often emerge as the recovering addict begins to discover his or her true self. This changes the dynamics of the relationship. It's as if a couple has learned the dance steps to the tune of addiction. And although they're not crazy about the dance itself, it's become a familiar routine. When that song stops playing and the new tune starts—one that follows the beat of recovery—the couple can feel lost. They don't know the steps to this new dance. They don't know how to relate to each other under these new conditions. How are we going to struggle with our differences? What is sex going to be like? Is my partner still going to like me? Did we get together or marry for the right reason? These and other important questions are bound to surface. This is why a couple needs support to adjust to recovery, because if they don't learn a new dance step, they will insist on doing the old dance that didn't work and that might lead to a breakup and possibly relapse for the person or persons in recovery.

I worked with a couple whose destructive patterns of shame, recrimination, and acting out demonstrate how relationship trouble can offer clues to how to break out of the cycle of addiction. Evan was having a hard time staying sober. His wife, Martha, couldn't stop nagging him or trying to change him. When Evan got a period of sobriety, Martha's criticism shifted from focusing on his drinking to what she thought he should be doing around the house or how he wasn't going to enough AA meetings or how he didn't call his sponsor. She nagged him and criticized him whenever she had the opportunity.

When Martha behaved like this, Evan started out responding like a little boy who desperately wanted to please his angry mother. But his contrition didn't last long. Eventually he became sick and tired of her complaining and micromanaging. He became resentful and would drive to the nearby liquor store, buy alcohol, and get drunk. He would sit at home drunk, and when Martha walked in the door after a long day at work, he'd unleash his rage and tell her how sick and tired he felt of her criticism and her efforts to control him.

His drinking was a misguided and feeble attempt to hold on to his sense of self and personal dignity, but the attempt came with a very high price: Evan lost his self-respect and integrity, and he lost Martha's respect. He felt intense shame and guilt, which fueled the cycle of self-punishment and active addiction all over again.

For Evan, the trouble was caused by his inability to hold on to his sense of who he was. He needed to relate to his wife as an adult, rather than responding as a pleasing or deviant child. When she talked to him like a critical parent, he responded like a guilty or angry little boy. He acted out by either trying to please her or hurt her. Both responses are sides of the same coin: they're the actions of an insecure child who is afraid of his mother's disappointment. Evan didn't know how to respond to Martha as an adult when he was being treated like a child. He became the emotionally dependent child, even as he pleaded with her to stop treating him like a child. He tried to change her rather than becoming the adult he was asking her to see.

Martha, on the other hand, related to Evan as a scolding and shaming parent. She talked down to him like he was a child—even when he was telling her he needed to be treated like an adult. Both

Martha and Evan seemed to lack the skills to relate to each other as equal adults: they couldn't give up their old parent-and-child dance that they'd learned while Evan was using. The kind of trouble that Evan and Martha were having in their marriage was an invitation. It was inviting them to learn how to relate to each other from the adult ego state, to learn a new dance step. It was inviting them both to learn to hold on to their sense of self while being in conflict.

When you have trouble in your relationship, it doesn't mean that something is wrong with your recovery. Conflict is a natural part of being in a committed relationship and can be an invitation to learn new steps in your relationship dance—especially if you are still trying to do the old dance you learned when you were still drinking or using. And if you can't figure out what the invitation is about, or you realize you're having trouble holding on to your sense of who you are, then ask for help from a marriage or family counselor.

Summary: Are Toxic Attitudes Limiting Your Recovery?

We have explored several toxic attitudes in this chapter—myths and flawed assumptions that can wreak havoc in our lives. If these harmful attitudes are not questioned and replaced with more nourishing ones, they will eventually sabotage your recovery.

If you are having trouble in your recovery, ask yourself and answer the following questions:

- What part of my problem is caused by a toxic attitude?
- What role are my unrealistic beliefs and expectations playing?
- What role are my fears playing?
- What part of my problem is caused by my avoidance?

- What aspect of my problem is caused by my insistence that I have to be right?
- What aspect is caused by my emotional dependency?
- Is my passivity contributing to the difficulty I am having?
- What role is my need to control playing?
- What part of my problem is caused by my lack of faith in my ability to be flexible and grow?

If you can't put your finger on what you are doing to contribute to the problem you are having, get some help from your sponsor, a trusted loved one, or a counselor. You can't see what you can't see.

As you have learned, the toxic attitudes listed in this chapter can carry with them the idea that you shouldn't need help, or that you can't face the painful truths (or become the capable self) that might help bring about necessary changes in your recovery. If this applies to you, try to put those ideas aside long enough to get the help you need.

In the next chapter we'll see how devious we can be when avoiding ourselves and pretending to be someone that we are not.

Stupid Thing 10

Donning a White Robe and Halo When You Need to Be Digging in the Muck

The spirituality to be discovered and uncovered through working the Twelve Steps offers a remarkable way of life. But believing that you don't need to deal with personal issues because you have found an all-encompassing "spiritual solution" to your problems—a spiritual bypass—is simply a way to avoid the, at times, painful, difficult, and muddy work of self-discovery and healing.

I used to coordinate a monthly seminar here in Southern California called "The Unfolding Self in Recovery." My co-facilitator was Teresa Tudury, an amazing woman who had been on her own personal spiritual journey for several decades. Her contribution to the seminar was far-reaching. In addition to bringing her penetrating insights about the topics we were discussing, she also shared her gifts of song and humor, her remarkable voice, and lyrics that fully capture the human condition.

Teresa had an interesting background. She was the songstress for Marianne Williamson, the bestselling author of several books derived from *A Course in Miracles,* a self-study spiritual program that has attracted thousands of adherents, including many Twelve Steppers, since its publication in 1975. Teresa shared an epiphany she'd had during the time she spent with *A Course in Miracles.* Her reflection made me stop and think about my own relationship to my spirituality.

She told us that she'd reached a point where she was using her spirituality to avoid dealing with life. When I first heard her share this idea, it seemed heretical. In my own absolutist habit of thought, I'd assumed that spirituality could only have positive outcomes as a way of coping better with life. How could it be used to avoid dealing with one's humanity or recovery?

One of the many things I love about Teresa is her sense of humor. She has a way of looking at things that simultaneously makes us laugh and recognize something about ourselves that we needed to see. She once noted that during her spiritual journey she had become so enlightened that she forgave others before they even stepped on her foot. This was hilarious, but it also pinpointed my own immature idea of spirituality.

I had secretly wished that spirituality would be a panacea for everything that ailed me. It would magically elevate me above the struggles I had in life. Even more outrageous, I hoped spirituality would turn me into the self that I thought I should be—a transformation that would, of course, solve all my problems.

As Teresa helped me learn, sometimes we lean on our spiritual tools to avoid pain and suffering, just like we used alcohol and other drugs. The truth was, I didn't want to grow up. I didn't want to face the person I had become. I was using an immature understanding of spirituality to justify avoiding the issues that were surfacing in my recovery. This was another form of avoidance, the defense mechanism we discussed earlier. Avoidance kept up the delusion that I was someone I was not. Avoidance kept me from facing some very painful experiences in my life.

Avoidance was a familiar friend, although I wouldn't admit it. Throughout my life I'd routinely avoided suffering or discomfort—a large factor in my alcohol use. From my early adolescence to my young adulthood and even during the early years of my recovery, I turned avoidance into an art form.

Spiritual Bypass

Because we consistently practice sidestepping our discomfort or pain, it becomes an automatic response, a habitual way of functioning. When avoidance manifests itself in the context of our spirituality and recovery, it's called a *spiritual bypass.* This is usually toxic to our full recovery because it interferes with our personal transformation. Dr. Ingrid Mathieu's *Recovering Spirituality* (2011) was the first book to discuss spiritual bypass as it relates to recovery in AA, and it remains a valuable resource. But those of us who suffer from addiction haven't cornered the market on using spirituality to avoid dealing with ourselves. This tendency has been observed and discussed by several noteworthy spiritual teachers and psychotherapists.

In his book *Toward a Psychology of Awakening,* John Welwood defined spiritual bypassing as

> . . . using spiritual ideas and practices to sidestep personal, emotional "unfinished business," to shore up a shaky sense of self, or to belittle basic needs, feelings, and developmental tasks, all in the name of enlightenment. (2002, p. 207)

Can you see how problematic a spiritual bypass would be in Stage II recovery? It is during this phase of recovery that the issues we have been avoiding usually come to the surface. In fact, I tell my clients that when long-buried issues surface in this phase of recovery, it doesn't mean something is wrong. Quite the opposite! It indicates that something is *right* about our recovery. Because our sense of self is growing, we are now ready to face the many issues we've been avoiding.

Bill Wilson knew that we had to face who we had become in order to move toward the self we truly are. When discussing Step Five in *Twelve Steps and Twelve Traditions,* he wrote, "To those who have made progress in A.A., it amounts to a clear recognition of what and who we really are, followed by a sincere attempt to become what we could be" (Alcoholics Anonymous, 1981, p. 58).

Luther's story: Spirituality as avoidance

Luther, a client of mine, comes to mind. He had been sober for three years when he began seeing me for psychotherapy. Our first meeting was most unusual; he began by telling me he wasn't certain why he was seeing me. He went on to tell me that his life was better than ever. He had three years of sobriety, his job was secure, his health was good, he wasn't depressed or anxious, and his desire to drink and use had been lifted. The one thing that was missing in his life was a relationship.

At forty-two, Luther had never been in a committed relationship. He didn't start dating until college, and none of his dates seemed to amount to anything serious. He was confused. He said that on paper he looked great. He was of average appearance, quite successful in his line of work, attended church on a regular basis, and his one bad fault, his drinking, was being addressed. "I just don't understand. Why aren't women interested in me?" he asked in a tone that also pleaded, "Help me—I am terribly lonely." (Interestingly, he hadn't identified loneliness as a reason he was seeking help.)

I asked him to describe the last date he'd had in as much detail as he could remember. He went on to describe the most boring evening one could imagine. Luther was so shut down and out of touch with his feelings that there wasn't much of him there to connect to. It was no surprise that this woman wouldn't want to see him again. I pointed this out, but oddly, my observation didn't seem to bother him. I was curious about his air of indifference.

As we explored his reaction to my feedback, it became clear that he prided himself on what he called his "independence." He didn't *want* to need anyone or ever depend on another human being. I probed deeper and learned that his mother was quite domineering. She controlled him and his father, and always seemed to consume all the oxygen in a room. To cope, his father withdrew from her demands. The parents rarely communicated; Luther's father just complied as much as he could or avoided interactions altogether. With this as a model for how relations between men and women work, Luther determined that his best bet was not to expose much of his inner self. He concluded that one could not be independent when in a relationship. In other words, he had no models of a healthy relationship, one in which both partners hold on to their sense of self while also being part of a loving, supportive relationship.

Interestingly, Luther told me that he depended on God and claimed that his strong spiritual program had helped him rise above the needs and desires most people have, and for that he was happy. It seemed to me that he was proud of that fact. "Emotions are complicating factors in life, and I've done much better since I've erased my needs and emotions," he said.

I pointed out to him how objective he sounded, and that it seemed like he had forgotten how to let himself really *need or want* something. This observation seemed to pique his interest. Like many damaged people, Luther had lost interest in himself and settled for a half-lived life. He had forgotten—or perhaps had never learned—how to listen to the desires and drives of his true self.

He was also using his dependence on his relationship with God to avoid addressing—to bypass—the needs and emotions that made him a unique human. He had created a safe cocoon to live in, but there wasn't room in it for a woman. There was only room for Luther and his brand of spirituality, and he was becoming quite lonely.

He was terrified of being consumed and lost in a relationship—which was understandable, given his history. He defended against this fear by using his spirituality to reinforce the idea that he had no emotional needs or wants—he was a kind of saint, devoid of all worldly interests. He thought that he could live his life free of desire, but this left him feeling like an empty shell incapable of being in an intimate relationship.

The truth is that a part of Luther had buried the pain of witnessing his parents' relationship, where the only options were to dominate and control, or clam up and be "independent." This long-buried pain was emerging, and it manifested as the growing loneliness that brought him to see me. We need other people—it's that simple. The emergence of Luther's recognition of this need was a good sign that he was ready to begin Stage II recovery and develop a healthy spirituality that allowed for the messy needs and emotions that a committed relationship calls up.

Luther worked hard with me for the next couple of years and focused on dealing with his unfinished business with his parents. Then he focused on developing the ability to stay true to himself while being connected to someone he cared about. It was tough going for a long time. He became quite anxious for some time, which he hated, but he hung in there, found a partner, and learned that he could have a healthy relationship while holding on to his true self and practice a more mature spirituality. At this writing, he's been married for five years.

Healthy and Unhealthy Spirituality

John Battista, my supervisor and instructor at the University of California–Davis, discussed the difference between what he called healthy or true spirituality and unhealthy or false spirituality. He described healthy spirituality as "spiritual practices and beliefs that further the development and transformation of personality" (1996, p. 251). This is what we strive for in recovery. Unhealthy spirituality, he said, is "spiritual practices and beliefs that have been incorporated into a psychopathological personality" (1996, p. 251).

Clearly Luther had been practicing unhealthy spirituality—using spiritual methods to maintain isolation and avoid the kind of human contact that would ultimately enable his personal transformation. Luther's spirituality was really a form of avoidance. But keep in mind that Luther probably wasn't ready for change until he found his way to a therapist who could help him unlock the painful family history he was avoiding.

This brings us to an important point. True, a spiritual bypass, if clung to forever, is unhealthy, since it blocks transformation. But using a spiritual bypass isn't always destructive, as long as it doesn't become a permanent solution. Luther likely needed the time to get sober, and his loneliness then became the ultimate driver to help him seek further change. Let's look at another example.

Jane's story: Benefitting from a temporary spiritual bypass

Jane was referred to me by her second sponsor, Gloria, who was concerned that the Step work they were doing wasn't enough to help her overcome the depression and anxiety she was experiencing after several years of sobriety. Her sponsor recognized that Jane was suffering terribly and needed more help than she could get from the AA program and her sponsor.

When we met, I learned that Jane was the victim of childhood incest, which lasted for nearly a decade. Her uncle molested her from age six through sixteen. When she finally told a teacher about it, the teacher reported the child abuse to the proper authorities and her uncle was arrested, tried, and sent to prison.

This was her father's older brother. He was everybody's favorite uncle and many of Jane's relatives couldn't believe he was capable of this unthinkable behavior. So they turned on her: she was shunned and shamed by his side of the family. Some went so far as to openly accuse her of making the whole story up so she would get attention. That was bad enough, but even worse, her father didn't support her and challenge their nonsense. He fell silent. He stood by and watched his family shame his daughter and did nothing about it.

Jane's mother supported her behind closed doors but never openly during these confrontations with her father's family. Her mother's half-hearted protection, combined with her father's utter lack of support, deeply traumatized Jane. She felt betrayed by her uncle, her father's family, her father, and to a large extent her mother. She had suffered multiple traumas as a child. It was no wonder that she was depressed and angry and having nightmares.

When Jane had started attending AA meetings six years earlier, she was drinking almost a fifth of vodka a day. Her detox was difficult, and it took almost a year before the toxic effects of the alcohol on her body and brain started to resolve. From year two to four in the program, she stayed in the background, frightened and unsure that AA was the right place for her.

She reflected back on this time and told me she just didn't trust anyone who claimed to be acting in her best interest. This was fallout from her trauma; to justify what he was doing, her uncle had told her over and over while he was molesting her, "You are a very lucky young girl to get this special attention from me."

In AA, Jane eventually reached out to Nancy, a self-appointed AA spiritual guru, to be her first sponsor. Nancy believed that you couldn't have a fit spiritual program unless you forgave those who had hurt you. Indeed, forgiveness is an important part of recovery. It helps us evict those people we resent from living rent-free in our heads. But forgiveness can't be willed into being. Rather, it is the result of an often complex process that involves developing a new narrative and perspective about what happened.

Nancy didn't fully understand the psychological process of forgiveness. She created a spiritual bypass by fusing spirituality with forgiveness. Nancy worked with Jane for over a year on forgiving her uncle and the other family members who had betrayed her, suggesting that she pray for them. Jane conscientiously prayed for them and started to believe that she had forgiven them, and had therefore fulfilled Nancy's requirement that she release them and all of her resentment and pain.

While not really resolving Jane's trauma, Nancy had still helped her come to terms with it temporarily until she was ready to dig into the deep pain and anger. At the time, Jane couldn't tolerate the intensity of these emotions because she hadn't yet developed a solid sense of her true self. Nancy used a form of spiritual bypass to help Jane begin to address her avoidance of the trauma and prepare her for the work she would need to do in the future to get to a deeper and more emotional level of resolution and forgiveness.

Jane's experience shows that sometimes a spiritual bypass can be beneficial until someone develops a stronger sense of self. This was the surprising insight that Ingrid Mathieu discovered in her research on spiritual bypass in recovery.

> Adaptive experiences of spiritual bypass can provide you with a sense of protection from relapse and a safeguard from emotions that might be too overwhelming to feel at a particular time. . . . So using spiritual practices or ideas defensively can be a useful experience in recovery: a person can maintain physical sobriety long enough for deeper issues to be addressed at a later time. (2011, p. 167)

This was indeed the case for Jane. Her spiritual bypass of intellectually adopting Nancy's model and "acting as if" she had forgiven her family for its terrible betrayal enabled Jane to get physically sober and gradually develop a stronger sense of self. So by the time she had come to see me, she was ready to go deeper and give voice to the anger and pain she had buried since the time of the trauma.

It was quite clear that Jane had never felt safe or on solid enough ground to express these feelings she had carried for the past thirty years of her life. Nancy had provided temporary help but had also delayed Jane's healing by advising her to bypass her pain and anger and prematurely encourage forgiving her family.

Somewhere in her fourth year of recovery, Jane started having nightmares. She wasn't able to remember much about these dreams, but she did recall that she was being chased and was terrified that she'd be caught and have to face whatever was chasing her. Some emotions were beginning to surface for Jane, and it really shook the foundation of her recovery. Nancy continued to try to help her, but her approach to the problem no longer met Jane's needs. Jane was ready to face her trauma at a deeper level, and she needed a different kind of help to do that.

It was a struggle for Jane to end the sponsorship relationship with Nancy, but she knew she needed more help than Nancy was able to give. In year five of her recovery Jane met another sponsor, Gloria, a warm and loving woman who had been successful in working with women who had been traumatized. Gloria never pushed these women to confront their traumas until they were ready, but she had an uncanny way of helping them get ready. I had already successfully helped several of Gloria's sponsees who had been deeply traumatized in their childhood, so she referred Jane to me. Jane was ready when she walked into my office. All of the feelings she had been avoiding broke loose and flowed during our sessions. A dam had shattered inside of her, releasing the river of the thoughts and feelings she had been holding back.

By way of the empty chair technique I described earlier, we invited all of the members of her family into the session one by one so she could let them know all the things she had dared not say. We started with her uncle and worked her way through the list. Interestingly, the most difficult person to confront was her mother. But she eventually found the words that most accurately expressed the resentment, grief, and anger that she had repressed for so long. She was able to forgive some of her family members; for others, she declared her right to never forgive them but to let them go—from her head and from her heart.

This process relieved her of her depression and anxiety, and her nightmares stopped. Today she helps other women in the program who were also molested. Every now and again she pops back in for a tune-up, but the work she did has helped her deepen her recovery, and get and stay grounded. She is now confident in her ability to deal with her emotions.

Depression and anxiety may be signaling that we have some unfinished business that needs to be taken care of. Psychologist Fritz Perls put it this way:

> The enemy of development is pain phobia—the unwillingness to do a tiny bit of suffering. You see, the pain is a signal of nature. The painful leg, the painful feeling, cries out, "Pay attention to me—if you don't pay attention things will get worse." (1969, p. 52)

You can see that Jane had been suppressing her feelings, and that they had exerted great pressure to be released. Though some people might think that Jane should have made dealing with her trauma her first priority, she wasn't ready. She needed to get sober first, and the spiritual bypass provided by Nancy helped her paper over the trauma enough to stay sober. Once she had enough sobriety, the pressure of the blocked feelings grew and grew. Fortunately, she found a safe place to express them (a therapist's office) and began recovery on her terms, including forgiving members of her family, or not, as she felt was right. This opened the door for her real spiritual journey.

Peter and Helen's story: Spiritual defensiveness

Another way of avoiding ourselves by using unhealthy spiritual practices is called *spiritual defensiveness.* Dr. Battista defined it in this way: "Spiritual defenses provide a rationale to disavow parts of one's self" (1996, p. 252).

Earlier, we discussed the unfortunate practice of disowning a part of ourselves when we mistakenly equate development and care of self with selfishness. That's all too common in Twelve Step recovery. And that's what happened with my client, Peter. I met Peter when he was six months sober. He had a serious problem with Vicodin, Xanax, and alcohol. He'd gone to a major treatment center and responded very well to its program. His wife joined him for a week in the family program, and it was very powerful for both of them. He really opened his ears and heart to hear and feel her pain and anxiety. It was the most intimacy they'd experienced for a number of years, and they were eager to continue their reconciliation when he returned home.

They contacted me three months after Peter left treatment. The honeymoon period was over; there was a growing tension and alienation between them. And they couldn't put their finger on what had happened.

Initially things had been great. Peter and Helen spent a lot of time talking, and he became the "perfect" husband. He tried to meet all of his wife's needs, trying to make up for the years he'd been lost in his addiction and neglecting her. She was all too eager for this attention and nurturing, and she was enjoying soaking it all up.

But after several months of this, Peter started to become sarcastic and irritable. He'd say things like "I didn't think recovery would turn me into a slave." He started resenting her requests and eventually exploded, calling Helen selfish and demanding. This wounded her deeply. They were in trouble and didn't know what to do, so they turned to me for help. This time they couldn't blame their marital problems on Peter's active addiction.

The first session was intense. Helen was very hurt and bitter. Peter was resentful and felt that Helen didn't appreciate all he had been doing. To calm things down I decided to give Peter and Helen a talk about how we're always balancing two forces in a marriage, the desire for togetherness and the need to honor our individuality. I wanted to give them both a perspective that might help them navigate their way through troubled waters, to get them to step back and look at their problems more objectively instead of reacting defensively and impulsively.

I explained that conflict in a relationship was a way of negotiating the level of intimacy that was going to exist in the relationship.

Every relationship balances each partner's need for togetherness with their need for individuality. In a healthy relationship, these are in balance: you have union while preserving individuality. Discord in a relationship often indicates an imbalance; to some degree, either individuality or togetherness has been lost.

Because Peter wanted to recover from his addiction, be a better partner, and make up for all the grief and pain he'd caused Helen, he mistakenly believed that he had to be completely self-effacing, that he had to disavow any display of self, which he equated with selfishness. He mistakenly believed that this was a part of the spiritual solution to his problem.

Peter's sponsor had taught him that self-centeredness was the root of his addiction and caused many of his marital problems. Therefore Peter decided that he needed to make up for his selfishness in the past by putting his wife's needs ahead of his own. He was using the spiritual concept of the martyr who sacrifices everything for others to cover up his inability to balance his need to express his true self.

But not knowing how to take care of ourselves actually makes us more selfish. When we learn to balance our desire and need for cooperation and belonging with our need to be our true selves and grow as individuals, we strengthen our connection with each other and build a relationship based on trust and mutual support. The only way I can truly honor your needs is if I am truly honoring my own needs. Dr. Walter Kempler, my mentor, put it this way:

> I can only be responsible to and for myself and there it ends. This thought frightens many people and the word anarchy comes to mind. Responsibility to and for oneself, on the contrary, produces greater commitment

> for others. We cannot give what we do not have. (1981, p. 37)

As Peter and Helen found, this kind of balancing can sometimes require ditching the halo and getting down into the muck, facing how our addict self is still playing a role in our relationships. When we do, we can have genuine connection with others based on meeting the mutual needs of our true or spiritual selves.

Here are a few sentences to complete related to these issues.

- Balancing my needs with my partner's needs means . . . .
- The role that spirituality plays in my recovery is . . . .
- I play the martyr when I . . . .
- Being spiritual means . . . .
- I use my spiritual practice to avoid . . . .
- The hardest thing about balancing my desire to cooperate with my need for individuality is . . . .
- For me, getting down in the muck means . . . .
- I use my Twelve Step program to avoid . . . .

Summary: Digging in the Muck

When a patient of mine is ambivalent about addressing a painful issue, I offer this reminder: "You can pay me now or pay me later." We can try to avoid digging in the muck, but eventually the issue we've been avoiding is going to surface. *It is going to show up in our lives through our dreams or through the patterns that occur in our relationships.* We are wired to complete unfinished business, to move toward wholeness—or, as some say, (w)holiness. To be fully recovered from addiction we must realize and embrace our potential.

The way I see it, all approaches to recovery help us recover our lost true self. We can call this our higher self or spiritual self—these terms are all synonymous. *Our problem was that at some point we rejected our true self to become the self that we thought we should be—which sets us up for an addict-self takeover when our brains are hijacked by addiction.* This is our false self, which is what is really meant when ego is discussed in the Twelve Step literature.

We dedicated our lives to actualizing a concept of who we *should* be rather than actualizing the self we truly *are*. Our true self, you see, consists of the interplay of the desire and need to belong and cooperate (togetherness), and the desire and need to march to our own drum (individuality). When we operate from our true self, we strive to balance both of these desires. When these two are in balance, we can be self-concerned without being self-centered, self-aware without being selfish. This is what allows us to show genuine concern for others and fulfill the spiritual goal of service suggested by Step Twelve. Operating from our true self is the hallmark of emotional sobriety.

Fritz Perls understood that avoidance of suffering was at the root of our trouble. He observed that "we are phobic, we avoid suffering, especially the suffering of frustrations. We are spoiled, and we don't want to go through the hellgates of suffering: We stay immature, we go on manipulating the world, rather than to suffer the pains of growing up" (1969, p. 56).

Recovery is about learning how to deal with and grow from our suffering. Taking a spiritual bypass is believing that if we follow a particular spiritual path, we can avoid suffering. One thing I have learned in my own personal work, and in helping thousands of men and women, is that we are much more capable than we know. We have a remarkable ability to face our pain and go beyond it to reach our full potential. But we will never realize it if we betray ourselves by using avoidance mechanisms such as spiritual bypass to maintain a false self that keeps us from honestly assessing our capacity to deal with life as it is.

In the next chapter we'll explore the effects of insisting that life conform to our expectations and how this idea relates to the concept of emotional sobriety.

Stupid Thing 11

Insisting That Reality Conform to Your Expectations

Life presents us with its own terms, and our job is to learn to live with them. Failure to manage our expectations is a setup for unhappiness and relapse.

If you've read this book from the beginning, you may have noticed something I've said often: the *problem* is not the problem. Rather, the problem is how you *relate* to the problem. That's what this chapter is about—the nature of our "problems" in recovery.

I believe that many of the snags we encounter in recovery are ones we generate for ourselves. Sometimes they're not really problems at all. They arise because events, other people's actions and responses, and other parts of life unfold contrary to our wishes.

Sometimes our expectations are really crazy, such as the ones that arise from the stupid things we've discussed: expectations that we will never fail, that we won't have creeping thoughts of drinking or using again, that if we just follow some wiser person's directions, everything will be better, that we can get everything we need from the Twelve Step rooms. The list of unrealistic expectations goes on and on.

Sometimes our reactions to thwarted expectations create more new problems for us to deal with. So, for example, we may respond by becoming passive, failing to take responsibility for the direction of our lives or the way we react to events and people. We may respond by becoming angry, or running and hiding, or blaming. And so we create a snowballing avalanche of "problems," all related to our expectations, our response to those expectations, how other people respond to what we say or do, how we then respond to those people, and on and on and on. It is sad and a little absurd, if you think about it.

The goal of this chapter is to help you learn to sidestep this avalanche. Insisting that reality always conform to our expectations is perhaps the stupidest of the many stupid things we humans, and especially we addicts, do. Have you ever asked yourself why we have so many expectations—and why we have so many rules about how life is "supposed" to be? These two questions sound different, but in fact they are variations on the same theme, because they both relate to things that interfere with our emotional sobriety.

Expectations generate rules: unenforceable rules and claims on how things are supposed to be. These demands become a serious challenge for those of us looking to find a better way of life. Unpacking this problem is crucial to achieving the emotional sobriety that is necessary if we are going to enjoy long-term stable recovery.

Bill Wilson was the first to talk about emotional sobriety in a widely quoted 1956 letter he wrote answering a question from an AA member in California. Bill was asked to discuss how the Twelve Steps might help deal with depression. Given that Bill struggled with depression in his own recovery, he was eager to share what he had learned in his quest to understand and confront his own struggle. When he looked into his depression, Bill discovered that it was ultimately caused by his emotional dependency. He wrote:

> My basic flaw had always been dependence—almost absolute dependence—on people or circumstances to supply me with prestige, security, and the like. Failing to get these things according to my perfectionist dreams and specifications, I had fought for them. And when defeat came, so did my depression. (1988, p. 237)

Bill was able to see that he was dependent on people or circumstances for his emotional well-being and self-esteem. If people responded according to his "perfectionist dreams and specifications," or if a situation unfolded according to his expectations, he was all right. But if people didn't respond the way he wanted, or if a situation didn't unfold according to his expectations, he was knocked off balance. Bill tried to recover his balance by fighting to get his way, but when that didn't happen he felt defeated and deflated. He became depressed.

It would seem that being knocked off balance was Bill's problem, when in fact the real problem was that Bill didn't know how to regain his balance once he lost it. He didn't know how to recover his sense of emotional balance other than by trying to manipulate others or the situation. Bill suffered from the common toxic belief that our well-being depends on what other people say or do. We believe that our sense of security should come from how other people treat us and that our job is to please or manipulate them to control their reactions and responses. But if our sense of security is determined by regulating other people, we will never be safe or feel safe. We extend this toxic belief not just to people but to life circumstances in general. The fact is, stuff happens: we get sick, we are laid off, a loved one dies, our car is stolen, our partner asks for a divorce. The list of uncontrollable possibilities is endless. The key is to do what we can in every situation and let go of the rest. Undoing the toxic belief that life *shouldn't* be the way it is and that we *should* be able to control all the outcomes is one of the keys to achieving emotional sobriety. It's not that we don't let people or situations bother us or that we don't have feelings about getting knocked off balance at times. Rather it's that we develop the ability to regain our balance when it happens; we develop the resilience necessary for emotional sobriety.

Emotional sobriety is about keeping our *emotional center of gravity*. The best way to grasp this concept is to first understand what a physical center of gravity is and how it affects our behavior.

Our physical center of gravity is related to the physical mass of our body. It is the point in our body through which gravity travels toward the center of the earth. When the line of gravity falls outside of our base of support, then a reaction is needed to maintain our balance.

A low and balanced physical center of gravity means high stability. When I was in Vietnam, we were assigned two Korean Marines to teach us tae kwon do. One of the first stances we learned from these two skilled fighters was the horse stance. It's also called the immovable stance because the fighter drops his center of mass equally over both feet, creating a very solid, athletic base. When we were in this stance, it was hard for anyone to knock us off balance.

Our emotional center of gravity is similar. It is the point at which emotions pass through us to the center of our sense of self. When our sense of self is solid and yet flexible, and our emotional center of gravity is in tune with our true self, then we can trust our experience and ability to respond to life's challenges. We don't let people or circumstances knock us off balance. When, on the other hand, we position our emotional center of gravity outside ourselves, it is quite easy for us to trip. To illustrate this process, let me share with you a very profound experience my wife and I had.

When my wife, Jessica, got pregnant, she was a post-doctoral student at the University of California–Los Angeles. We decided to have our child with the help of the midwife practice at UCLA, a great group dedicated to helping women naturally deliver their babies. In the first trimester of her pregnancy, everything was normal. But because it was UCLA, we decided to participate in the genetic screening program. They first tested Jessica by drawing blood to screen for various genetic abnormalities. If she was normal, there would be no need to do further testing on me. So a month or so went by and all of the well-baby visits were unremarkable, which meant that mom and the baby were doing fine. But this was unexpectedly about to change.

We were attending a scheduled well-baby visit on a Monday morning and once again the midwife gave us her blessings and sent us on our way. "Everything looked fine!" she said. So my wife and I said our goodbyes, and she started walking back to her lab on campus. I jumped in the car and started driving down to South Bay to see clients. About twenty minutes into my commute I received an urgent call from Jessica. When I answered the phone, she could hardly speak to me between her tears and anxiety. She was panicked. I asked her what happened. She told me that the midwife had called her back to the office because she forgot to review the results from the genetic testing.

As it turned out, Jessica was a carrier of a particular kind of genetic disorder that could be devastating for an infant. If I also tested positive for this gene, then our child would have a 25 percent chance of being born with this genetic illness. In the worst case, this meant that our child—we had already determined she was a girl and had named her Maddy—would live approximately one and a half years and then die.

No parent wants to hear this kind of news. We certainly didn't.

In the best-case scenario, Maddy would live until she was in her early teens. She would never be able to function independently, and since this particular genetic illness prevents the lungs and the central nervous system from fully developing, she would be on life support her entire life. I can still remember seeing Jessica's face when I met her at the UCLA Medical Center. She was devastated, and when she informed me of what she had learned, we sat and cried. I had to give blood that day to determine if I also had this gene. But the test was so complicated that we wouldn't receive the results for several weeks. I thought, *Several weeks—are you kidding me!* How were we supposed to make it that long?

That night was horrible. We were flooded with fear, grief, anger, and anxiety. Neither of us slept much; we just lay in bed wrapped in our emotional pain.

We both imagined we would be spending the next several years watching our child suffer and feeling helpless to ease her pain. I started having crazy thoughts that God was punishing me for something I had done wrong in my life. There was certainly a long list of things God could have chosen from. I was knocked way off balance; I needed to find some way to recover my emotional footing, but I didn't know how. I called several friends and my sponsor, all of whom were very supportive and sympathetic, but that didn't help much. Yes, it was good to know they were there for me, but that didn't relieve the anxiety I had about the future. And then I began to realize that I was being held hostage by one of my expectations.

Like most parents, I had automatically expected to have a normal child. This is what I believed I needed to be okay with my life.

Now that I was facing the possibility that my daughter wouldn't be like most other children, I didn't know what to do. It was natural to be upset and anxious about something this serious, but my well-being had become dependent on her health and normality. I was lost and didn't know how to cope with life when it didn't adhere to my expectations.

I was knocked off balance; my emotional center of gravity was not centered in my thoughts and feelings. I was not in tune with my true self. I kept asking myself, What do I need to do to get my footing back? But nothing came to mind until midmorning the next day.

I have found that when I am not consciously thinking about the solution to a problem my unconscious mind continues to work on solving it. I have experienced this phenomenon several times in life. Sometimes when I was stuck struggling with a problem, I would sleep on it and the next day the solution would appear. Maybe God speaks to us best when our consciousness is not getting in the way.

Midmorning the next day I realized that I had given over all my power to the situation we were facing. The situation was determining how I was feeling. I let myself be taken hostage by my worst fears and my need to be in complete control of my life. I shared this idea with Jessica, and we began thinking about how we could take our power back. I started to realize that we had placed our emotional center of gravity in the situation rather than keeping it within us. Our emotional center of gravity needed to reside in our desire to be the best parents we could be.

All of a sudden I started asking questions: If Maddy is born with this problem, will I love her less? No, I won't! If she only survives for a year and a half, I will love her a lifetime while she's here. Tears started rolling down my cheeks. This was really empowering.

Once we decided that the situation wasn't going to control our feelings and our lives, we felt immense relief. Our anxiety dissipated;

we surrendered and were at peace. We had confidence in our ability to face whatever challenges life was going to offer.

Then I had another thought. I realized that Maddy wouldn't know the difference. Her life was her life, and it would be defined by how we felt about it, not by her condition. She wouldn't know what she was missing because this would be her reality. With this revelation we both reinforced our commitment to loving her regardless of her condition.

Do you see the freedom we had at that moment? We were no longer allowing ourselves to be held prisoners by our demands that life conform to our expectations. We had reconnected to our emotional center, which set us free from our anxiety and fear. The results of my genetic testing no longer mattered. We were free to love and enjoy Maddy as she was, not as we would like her to be.

Through this experience I felt firsthand the power of emotional sobriety, and the importance of challenging my expectations and examining my unenforceable rules and demands of life.

This is precisely what Bill Wilson encouraged us to do to achieve emotional sobriety. He wanted us to examine our reactions and unpack the forces that influence us to react in the manner we do. In his 1956 seminal letter to a depressed friend he wrote, "If we examine every disturbance we have, great or small, we will find at the root of it some unhealthy dependency and its consequent unhealthy demand."

My unhealthy demand was that Maddy, my unborn child, had to be normal. Well, who the heck am I to make this kind of demand on nature? My unhealthy dependency on events outside myself told me that I wouldn't be okay unless she was born normal. I made up this rule because I didn't have the faith in myself to cope with life on life's terms.

I had forgotten that our unenforceable rules regarding how things are supposed to be are an attempt to control the people and events surrounding us. We think that we need people to behave and events to happen in a certain way for us to be all right. We operate from an "I am okay if ______" consciousness instead of an "I am okay *even if* ______" consciousness. If we achieve this state of mind, then we will have a new level of emotional freedom; we will enjoy emotional sobriety.

If you'd like to learn more and take an Emotional Sobriety Inventory, I urge you to read my book on the subject, *12 Smart Things to Do When the Booze and Drugs Are Gone.* I've used Bill's concept to create an inventory form that will help unpack your reactions. By examining what underlies our reactions, we can begin to see our hidden unenforceable rules and the unhealthy dependency that is generating them.

As I've researched this subject, I realized that what Bill discovered in his recovery has been discussed by several prominent psychologists such as Karen Horney, Fritz Perls, and Virginia Satir, as well as Viktor Frankl, who we'll get to know further in the next chapter. Dr. Frankl discovered some important psychological principles when he was in the concentration camps in Nazi Germany. He was asking what kind of attitude it took to survive this horror. This is what he discovered:

> We had to learn ourselves and, furthermore, we had to teach the despairing men, that *it did not really matter what we expected from life, but rather what life expected from us*. We needed to stop asking about the meaning in life, and instead to think of ourselves as those who were being questioned by life—daily and hourly. Our answer must consist, not in talk and meditation, but in right action and in right conduct. Life ultimately means taking the responsibility to find the right answer to its

> problems and to fulfill the tasks which it constantly sets for each individual. (1984, p. 85)

My wife and I were faced with the dilemma that Dr. Frankl described so eloquently. You see, it did not matter what we expected from life, we were faced with what life presented to us. We were questioned by life, and initially we couldn't find a good answer. But eventually we discovered how to hold on to ourselves and take responsibility for what we could control—our attitudes and actions.

I am often asked how things turned out. The truth is, it wouldn't have mattered, because of our change in attitude. But for those of you who need an "end" to the story, my test came back negative. I didn't have the genetic mutation, so the probability that Maddy would be born with this debilitating illness changed dramatically in her favor. She was born healthy and amazes me on a daily basis with her love for life. I love her deeply and cherish every moment we share.

Let's let Bill Wilson sum it up for us.

> Sobriety is only a bare beginning, it is only the first gift of the first awakening. If more gifts are to be received, our awakening has to go on. And if it does go on, we find that bit by bit we can discard the old life—the one that did not work—for a new life that can and does work under any conditions whatever. Regardless of worldly success or failure, regardless of pain or joy, regardless of sickness or health or even of death itself, a new life of endless possibilities can be lived if we are willing to continue our awakening (1988, p. 234).

This is what we are discovering as we trek the path of recovery. We are given a path to an enlightened consciousness that opens the doors to living a full and meaningful life. But it doesn't just happen. No one is coming to make it happen for us. We have to step up, take action, and suffer the pain and discomfort that is part of the journey. We have to learn how to hold on to ourselves and lick our own wounds. We have to create the causes of the effects we desire.

This enlightened consciousness is forged out of our struggles, out of our pain, and out of facing life on life's terms. Don't sell yourself short. You are much more capable of tolerating pain and learning from it than you realize. If you need help, don't hesitate to ask for it. We have to take action, but there's a lot of help out there to support us as we learn to stand on our own two feet.

In previous chapters, I've asked you some questions to help you incorporate the concepts into your life. I have only one question for you in this chapter, but you will need to think hard about it:

- What problems am I creating through my expectations that reality conform to my desires?

Summary: "I'm okay *even* if . . ."

Let's surrender our expectations about how things should be and how others should behave. Life is what it is; how we cope with life is what really matters. This is the core concept of emotional sobriety. Surrendering your expectations leads to emotional freedom and maturity. With this as a foundation for your recovery, it doesn't really matter what happens to you. What matters most is how you respond and cope with it. This means that you can get and stay sober under any conditions: whether the climate is adverse or supportive, positive or negative, understanding or judgmental, forgiving or unforgiving, informed or misinformed, loving or indifferent. We grow out of an "I'm okay if" status to "I'm okay *even* if" status. We learn to stay balanced and grounded, and to soothe ourselves when we are disappointed or suffer a loss.

In the final chapter we will explore an important ingredient in self-actualization and help you understand the importance of sharing what you have been so freely given.

Stupid Thing 12

Working Only the First Eleven Steps and Not Integrating Service Work into Your Recovery

Service work—helping others through loving action—takes time and effort, and is a key to long-term sobriety, emotional health, and self-actualization.

Recovery—achieving physical *and* emotional sobriety—requires a major shift in the way we deal with ourselves. This makes sense, doesn't it? How can we stop being self-destructive without changing? We can't! To enjoy quality recovery and the full benefits of sobriety, we learn to behave and think differently in all areas of our life.

In the previous chapters we have discussed several ways that our consciousness and behavior have to change to support recovery. We have looked into the deleterious effects of passivity, we've explored toxic attitudes and how they sabotage our recovery, and we've seen that we are a population of various selves that need to work in harmony with each other. We've seen how "leaving ourselves out" by ignoring our experience undermines our growth. We've also discussed our need to pay attention to the warnings from our addict self to better recognize and nourish our recovery self; our true self.

A saying attributed to Albert Einstein is relevant here: "You cannot solve a problem with the consciousness that created the problem." We need to develop a new consciousness, one that resists the destructive forces of our addiction and disrupts the programming of our false self to liberate the constructive forces of our true self.

The Twelve Steps of Alcoholics Anonymous provide a methodology and technology that help create this kind of change. This powerful program systematically shatters our reliance on our false self and deconstructs the control of our addict self. It restores our sense of integrity, justice, and trustworthiness; ultimately, the Steps transform our addict self into our recovery self. (For a full list of the Twelve Steps, see the appendix of this book.) In addition to developing a new relationship with ourselves and others, there's another part of us that we need to respect, too, if we are going to fully enjoy recovery. This is a part of us that we lost sight of during our addiction—a part of us that needs to be integrated into our recovery if we are ever going to realize our full potential. We need to find a purpose for our lives.

Each and every one of us needs to feel that we are making a difference, that our lives have significance, that we are of value. This desire to be of value needs to be honored and fulfilled. For those of us in Twelve Step recovery, one of the essential ways this is realized is through being of service—to other alcoholics and addicts, our loved ones, and our community. This is the essence of the work that takes place in Stage III recovery.

Stage III Recovery

Stage III recovery is about self-actualization. It's about using all the tools we've acquired in recovery to live a meaningful and purposeful life. In this stage, we begin to fully realize our potentialities.

Stage III recovery is the focus of Steps Eleven and Twelve. These two Steps help us realize our full potential as a human being or, as some say, as a "spiritual being who is having a human experience." Let's discuss these two Steps and their effects on our lives.

> *Step Eleven:* Sought through prayer and meditation to improve our conscious contact with God *as we understood Him,* praying only for knowledge of His will for us and the power to carry that out.

This Step is grounded in an ongoing pledge to continue to evolve, mature, and learn about our true purpose in life. We begin to see that life is not about all the things we *have.* It's not about "getting more stuff," as the late George Carlin reminded us in his classic comedy routine. Life is about finding a balance between what we have and who we are. In fact, we realize that the more we give emotionally and spiritually, the more we actually have. This is a truth we have lost sight of during our active addiction. Step Eleven helps us honor the side of us that anchors our self-esteem in who we really are—our spiritual self—not in our possessions and the outward success sought by our false self.

I believe that the therapeutic value of this Step is to expand our consciousness. An expanded consciousness helps us see our potential for understanding our life's meaning and for our relationships with other people and our Higher Power. It also enables us to tap into our resiliency—the ability to not just cope with life's problems but to embrace them as opportunities for growth. Recovery is the discovery of new possibilities for a full and purposeful life. This is the spirit of Step Eleven.

And it prepares us for the tasks we are charged with in the next Step.

> *Step Twelve:* Having had a spiritual awakening as the result of these steps, we tried to carry this message to alcoholics, and to practice these principles in all our affairs.

Step Twelve comes at the end of a rigorous process of making significant changes in how we behave and in how we think—about ourselves, other people, and life in general. These changes need to be integrated, woven into the fabric of our personality. When we integrate a principle or idea into our personality, it becomes available for us to use when we run into a situation where we can apply it for the greater good.

Integration ensures that this new way of life is anchored deeply in our personality. Integration is accomplished by "practicing these principles in all our affairs." Practice (in applying these principles) doesn't make perfect, but it makes them a natural part of who we are.

Practicing these principles daily also helps us integrate them into our personality on an ongoing basis as our life and circumstances change. At first we must consciously work to integrate the principles into our life, but once they are integrated, they become a part of us. So what happens is that first we work the Steps and then the Steps work us. These principles form the infrastructure of our new way of life—a way of life that is grounded in honesty, humility, integrity, compassion, and personal responsibility. But there is another component to this final Step that we must explore, because it is at the heart of the matter. Step Twelve urges us in part to"carry this message to alcoholics."

What about "carrying the message" is so important to this spiritual awakening that the previous eleven Steps have engineered? Being of service plays a key role in developing a spiritual life—so much so that this practice is promoted in almost every religion or spiritual practice. In fact, there is sound psychological reason that being of service is important in recovery.

The knowledge of this comes from an unexpected source, a so-called naturalistic experiment that occurred at Auschwitz and in the other Nazi concentration camps during World War II. During these dark times, men and women of all ages were confronted by unimaginable acts of cruelty and inhumanity. Their experience, as seen through the eyes of Viktor Frankl, will help us understand the reasoning behind including service work in Step Twelve and ultimately in the solution to addiction.

Dr. Frankl was a psychiatrist practicing in Vienna when he was taken prisoner by the Nazis. As number 119,104, he was put to work doing hard manual labor, building and repairing railroad tracks, and digging tunnels. Only during the last few weeks of his captivity did he act as a medical officer, providing aid to fellow prisoners.

Throughout his time in the camps, he asked himself the question, What is the difference between those who psychologically survive and those who don't? He wanted to understand resilience. What attitudes or beliefs would help someone cope with this horror? He believed the answer might help us better understand what it takes for anyone to cope better with life.

You'll recognize his answer as a running theme throughout this book. He discovered that it is our *relationship* to the experience we are having that determines our emotional well-being, that our emotional well-being was not predetermined by the situation. He went on to report that

> The way in which man accepts his fate and all the suffering it entails, the way in which he takes up his cross, gives him ample opportunity—even under the most

> difficult situations—to add a deeper meaning to his life. (1984, p. 76)

This powerful and very empowering concept has helped shape my thinking and my life. If this could be the outcome for a man or a woman in a concentration camp, then clearly we in recovery can also find deeper meaning in accepting our fate, in admitting our difficulty with alcohol and other drugs, and in owning that our lives have become unmanageable.

Dr. Frankl helps us see that it is possible to give meaning to our struggles and efforts in recovery if we cultivate the right attitude. He shows us that all the pain and suffering we experience can add deeper meaning to our lives instead of depressing and demoralizing us.

But we need help to turn our pain and our struggle with alcohol and other drugs into something meaningful. We need a formula that will help us digest our experiences in a healthy way, to separate the wheat from the chaff.

That is exactly the kind of help we receive when we work the Twelve Steps. In one sense we are taught the formula that turns lead into gold. This remarkable gift freed many of us from the bond of addiction and from the debilitating *I should have known better.*

Dr. Frankl further discovered that those men and women who were able to add deeper meaning to their lives did so to give themselves a purpose to live for. Focusing on honoring their purpose allowed them to tolerate the intolerable. So here was the formula: *those men and women who gave themselves to a purpose greater than themselves were more resilient than those who did not.*

He went on to say that the

> . . . true meaning of life is to be discovered in the world rather than within man or his own psyche. . . . I have termed this constitutive characteristic "the

> self-transcendence of human existence." . . . The more one forgets himself—by giving himself to a cause to serve or another person to love—the more . . . he actualizes himself. (1984, p. 115)

Here is the missing piece of the formula that we need to fully recover from this dreadful disease of addiction. Step Twelve gives us a new purpose in life—to carry this message to the person who is still suffering.

Our aspiration in life is to share what we have been so freely given with another alcoholic or addict who is suffering. We pass on what we have learned to actualize our true potential. A simple statement reminds us that "the more I give, the more I have." This is very different than the predominant cultural theme that says "The more I have, the more I am."

Frankl noted that "self-actualization is possible only as a side-effect of self-transcendence" (1984, p. 115). So this is the reason that service work is so important: without it, our growth and recovery would be incomplete. If, as I believe, the Twelve Steps help us recover our true self, then our recovery isn't complete until we truly find our purpose in life, which is grounded in our need to be of value. I believe that our inner wisdom knows that this is an important piece of the self-puzzle that needs to be put in place if we are going to be whole.

I want you to meet Anna. At sixty-two, she had recently celebrated over eight years of sobriety. She was working a pretty good program when she started to see me over five years ago, but something was missing. At first she couldn't put her finger on what that was, but eventually it became clear that she wasn't working Step Twelve. True, she had experienced a spiritual awakening, if by that we mean that she was looking at life through a new pair of glasses. She was dealing with relationship problems that she had avoided for decades and was beginning to see how self-effacing she was, constantly doubting herself and feeling insecure.

She was getting a firm grasp on these areas and had also started to reconnect with one of her sons who had written her off. But she was beginning to feel bored. This troubled her because boredom had been a problem for her before. She was stuck in her recovery. She couldn't find a purpose for her life. Her adult children were independent and didn't need her like they used to. Her husband was quite self-sufficient and didn't rely on her for much, cooking most of his own meals and following a strict exercise routine to keep his back loose and pain-free. She had a couple of grandchildren, but they were in preschool most of the time.

Anna was lost.

Her sponsor was encouraging Anna to raise her hand at the close of the AA meeting when they asked for those who were available to act as sponsors to raise their hands, but she wouldn't. Anna's residual low self-esteem made it difficult for her to believe that she had anything to offer anyone else. She was heading for a crisis, and if something didn't open up for her soon, it was highly likely that she would relapse.

I encouraged Anna to own her self-effacing attitude. This was easy for her. Here's what she said:

- "I don't have anything that anybody else would want."
- "I'm not very smart. Most of the people in the program are smarter than me. Who would want to listen to anything I have to say?"
- "It took me five years of on-and-off sobriety to get five sober years. That's not a very good track record."

- “My relationship with my husband isn’t very good. I can’t help anyone with their relationship.”

Anna was good at wiping herself out. But she’s not the only one I’ve seen who struggles with their sense of value and worth in recovery. In fact, this is a very common theme that surfaces when some of us move into this phase. “I don’t have much to offer” is what I often hear.

If this is our core belief, then we are going to balk when it comes to carrying the message. And this is exactly the place where Anna was stuck in her recovery.

In our sessions I began challenging Anna’s absolute thinking that was fueling her overgeneralizations and giving her false evidence to support her self-effacing attitude. I helped her see that she was overlooking one major thing that she had to offer. She was staying sober even though her life wasn’t perfect. This is a major accomplishment, but she couldn’t see it because she was so focused on who she wasn’t. For months I focused on making her aware of her self-effacing behavior every time it showed up in our discussions. Soon she was spotting it almost as quickly as I was.

The main point in her therapy was to help Anna engage in some process that would develop her confidence in working with others. When we explored what she felt good about, she identified that going to school was always something that she liked. This became a key to helping Anna get unstuck.

I suggested that she could kill two birds with one stone. She could go back to school, which she liked, and develop the confidence to help others. I suggested that she attend a certification program in alcohol and drug counseling. I pointed out to her that this would give her something she liked to do and therefore remove her boredom. Simultaneously, it would help her develop confidence in working with others. She was intrigued and signed up later that day.

She attended class regularly for one year and did well—she was a good student. But she was also learning a lot about addiction and counseling. When she finished the program, she decided to volunteer running a group that introduced newly sober women to the Twelve Steps. The first week she ran the group she was filled with doubt, but by the end of the first group all her doubt had dissipated and was replaced with joy and excitement. She loved it, and the women loved it, too.

At this writing, Anna has been running that same group every Wednesday morning for over three years, and it has made a significant difference in her life. She even looks younger. She loves the work and is sponsoring several other women in the program. Is Anna still self-effacing? Yes, but much less so. Her sense of self has grown tremendously, and she now lives her life with a purpose: to carry this message to the person who is still suffering from addiction.

Anna found her own path to being of service. But you don't have to become a sponsor or an addiction counselor to be of service. Twelve Step programs offer many opportunities.

- Hanging out after a meeting and helping a newcomer feel welcome.
- Cleaning up after a meeting or volunteering for a commitment as secretary, treasurer, literature person, or greeter.
- Giving someone a ride to a meeting or home afterward.
- Continuing to make amends to those you have hurt.
- Sharing your recovery story with others.
- Speaking at a meeting, jail, or rehab program.

- Helping your sponsor when he or she goes out on a Twelve Step call.
- Making a donation at a meeting.
- Giving your phone number to a newcomer.
- Sharing your experience, strength, and hope in a meeting.
- Buying a newcomer an important piece of literature.
- Speaking up if someone is being shamed in a meeting.
- Just staying sober.

If you are looking to get more involved in helping others, make certain you have the right attitude when you do. The right attitude is embodied in this important principle: we help others because it helps us. We don't do it with the expectation that they need to appreciate what we're doing for them, or that they should respond as we'd hope they would. We give what we have because we want to give it, and therefore the giving becomes our reward.

I asked my sponsor, Tom McCall, who I introduced earlier, to share his thoughts and comments on service.

> I personally never liked the term *service*. It always felt either cultish or political. There are more meaningful terms, like *love in action, paying it forward,* or *giving back*. These seem to be more descriptive than the word *service*. These suit me much better. But what new members will hear in the rooms is, "get into service, get involved, become a part of the program," rather than being passive and hanging out on the fringes of the group. This is an important aspect of our recovery. In fact I believe it is essential if we are to enjoy all the benefits of recovery.
>
> Service can take many different forms, from taking on a commitment in your home group like making coffee or

setting up chairs or greeting people at the door, to being a secretary of a group. Since the "group" is the central focus of the service structure, these tasks and others like them are without doubt what make the program work. This is because the primary purpose of every group is to carry the message.

There are other vital aspects of service, such as doing Twelve Step work and sponsorship. These are all loosely organized and personalized aspects of the program and are also an important part of recovery.

But there is an organizational part of the fellowship that involves service, too. Most people in AA or NA are first introduced to this at the group level when it has its business meeting to discuss managing the money collected, paying rent, purchasing refreshments, or discussing how to improve the meeting and its ability to carry the message. This is where solutions to problems confronting the group are brainstormed and where one sees a service structure in action as individual members take on responsibilities and hold service positions.

From here we can see that AA and NA requires a service structure that supports the entire fellowship, from local area assemblies to national and international conferences. The point here is the recovery fellowship would never have grown to where it is today without the personal selfless commitment from so many members.

Not everyone will want to get involved at this level of service, nor should they, but what is essential to long-term recovery is that the following spiritual principle is lived and practiced as a way of life: we can't keep what we have been so freely given unless we also freely give it back or pay it forward.

There is a very real danger that once we are free of the state of desperation we will start to fall into a state of complacency. This complacency creates a sort of a spiritual selfishness based on the attitude that says, "I got mine, now you go find out how to get yours." This spiritual selfishness occurs when we only focus on our needs, on our careers, or on our personal life, and we don't give back.

One of the undisputable truths about the nature of our disease is that it is rooted deeply in selfishness and self-centeredness. The chance of having a life that is content and meaningful has a lot to do with the degree to which we "get out of our selves." This is where service can be a valuable tool. It provides an opportunity to learn to serve without expecting or demanding a certain kind of response. In a way we are learning love without a price tag.

In the book *Alcoholics Anonymous,* ambition is defined as a sincere desire to live usefully and walk humbly under the grace of God. This is an important reframing of the word ambition. Most of us came into recovery feeling that we were completely useless as a human being. Creating a solid sense of self-worth is necessarily tied to how useful we become. Getting involved in service is a way we can start to realize that we have something to offer, that we are useful, and that our pain and suffering can be of value. Just having the willingness to show up and say yes to a request to be of service—no matter what—can be a big turning point in recovery for many of us.

Getting involved in the World Service structure in NA opened up a new world for me. It allowed me to learn about myself and others in ways I would never have had the opportunity to do otherwise. Learning to work with groups of people from different cultures, with all kinds of personalities and points of view, helped me understand more clearly than ever before that my perception or opinion isn't always the correct one. This was important step in my personal development. Being able to compromise for the good of the whole, instead of demanding my limited ideas be adopted, helped me develop flexibility and respect for others and their opinions. Knowing that I can think I am so right when I am actually wrong has been an extremely important lesson.

I used to keep a little quote by my phone: "People don't care how much you know until they know how much you care." Bill Wilson exemplified this the day he met Dr. Bob. The rest is history, our history, and our story is not yet over. Each one of us adds a new page or chapter to the great recovery book of one alcoholic/addict sharing with another the hope we have found and the miracles we have experienced.

To identify how you might be stopping yourself from getting more involved in the program along these lines, complete the following sentences and explore your answers with your sponsor, your therapist, or someone else you trust.

- I stopped myself from being of service to the newcomer by telling myself . . . .
- I am selfish in recovery when I . . . .
- To be of more service to others, I would have to give up the idea that I am . . . .
- I feel of value when I . . . .
- One thing I can do today to help the person who is still struggling from their alcoholism or their addiction is . . . .
- I can be of service to my loved ones and community by . . . .

Summary: Being of Service

Many men and women have found that being of service has made a substantial contribution to the quality of their recovery. This service will look and be different at different phases of your recovery. As my sponsor Tom reminded me early in my recovery, "You can't give someone something you don't have."

Until I started to grow in my recovery, the best I could do was to clean up or put the meeting room back in order after we met. As I worked the Steps and started to heal emotionally and spiritually, I had more to offer. My contribution and service grew with my recovery. Your contribution is important to the fellowship regardless of how pedestrian it seems to be. The sum of each and every thing that we do to be of service creates the fellowship. Each and every contribution makes the whole.

Let's look at some of the benefits to your personal development of "love in action" and "paying it forward."

- It will help us get right-sized. We will discover that while we are important we are not essential, that something is happening in the rooms that is much bigger than us.
- It will help us see how our suffering, pain, and ignorance can be of value to the person who is still suffering.
- We will realize that it's not what we have but who we are that is important.
- We will come to see that the greatest gift is to be who we are. What we know isn't as important as how much we care.
- We will come to value authenticity and speaking from the heart.
- We will realize what it means to be a fully functioning human being.

In summary, the Twelve Steps help us realize that we needed to first heal ourselves before we had something to give away. But they also acknowledge that we can be of value just by continuing to actualize and become our true self, remembering that our goal always is progress, not perfection.

Afterword

A Recipe for Change

This book has "Stupid Things" in its title for good reason—it is an exploration of stupid things we recovering people routinely do to make our own lives much harder than they need to be. But in reality, we need to appreciate our own stupidity. After all, isn't it our *expectation* that we always be smart, that we always have the answer, that makes these things stupid in the first place? These mistakes, these Stupid Things, are opportunities to learn and grow.

> *I am much smarter now that I know that I'm stupid—*
> *that I know what I don't know.*

I used to dread that people would someday discover how dumb and incompetent I secretly felt inside. I suffered terribly from the shame of not being who I thought I should be. Once I owned my stupidity, my imperfections, and stopped expecting that I—and the people around me—have all the answers, I was able to open myself to the compassion and forgiveness of my spiritual self.

Recovery is about the discovery of new possibilities. Change cannot be willed or programmed into our behavior. Rather, it is the result of how we encounter ourselves and struggle with who we really are. Many of us have taken the path of least resistance and we have avoided facing our pain and the pain we have caused others. Recovery begins when we take responsibility for our addict self. It's only then that our true self can emerge.

Fritz Perls had this to say about the process of change.

> As long as you fight a symptom, it will become worse. If you take responsibility for what you are doing to yourself, how you produce your symptoms, how you produce your illness, how you produce your existence—growth begins, integration begins. (1969, p. 178)

I hope you feel encouraged to face the issues you have been avoiding in recovery. We are all "stupid" in one way or another. Don't run from your ignorance. Embrace it! Once you do, you will discover new things about yourself and new possibilities in how to cope and, in the end, how to thrive.

In the introduction to this book, we saw that recovery is like taking an arduous hike and that it helps to understand the terrain and some of the challenges you'll face along the way. But regardless of how well prepared you are and how much you anticipate what might happen, there is no substitute for what you'll learn as you put one foot in front of the other—especially when the going gets tough.

Good luck on your trek. I wish you all the best and hope this book will contribute to you finding your way as you "trudge the Road of Happy Destiny."

References and Works Consulted

Alcoholics Anonymous. (1981). *Twelve steps and twelve traditions* (3rd ed.). New York: Alcoholics Anonymous World Services.

Alcoholics Anonymous. (2001). *Alcoholics Anonymous* (4th ed.). New York: Alcoholics Anonymous World Services.

Battista, J. R. (1996). Offensive spirituality and spiritual defenses. In B. W. Scotton, A. B. Chinen & J. R. Battista (Eds.), *Textbook of transpersonal psychiatry and psychology* (hardcover ed.). New York: Basic Books.

Berger, A. (2006). *Love secrets revealed: What happy couples know about having great sex, deep intimacy and a lasting connection.* With M. Palmer. Deerfield Beach, FL: Health Communications, Inc.

Berger, A. (2008). *12 stupid things that mess up recovery.* Center City, MN: Hazelden.

Berger, A. (2010). *12 smart things to do when the booze and drugs are gone.* Center City, MN: Hazelden.

Berger, A. (2012). *12 hidden rewards of making amends.* Center City, MN: Hazelden.

Bugental, F. T. (1978). *Psychotherapy and process: The fundamentals of an existential-humanistic approach.* New York: Random House.

Frankl, V. E. (1959, 1984). *Man's search for meaning: An introduction to logotherapy* (3rd ed.). New York: Simon & Schuster.

Greenwald, J. (1977). *Is this really what I want to do?* Pasadena, CA: Ward Ritchie Press.

Horney, K. (1950, 1991). *Neurosis and human growth: The struggle toward self-realization.* New York: W. W. Norton.

Jacobs-Stewart, T. (2010). *Mindfulness and the twelve steps: Living recovery in the present moment.* Center City, MN: Hazelden.

Kempler, W. (1981). *Experiential psychotherapy within families.* CA: Kempler Institute.

Larsen, E. (1985). *Stage II recovery: Life beyond addiction.* New York: HarperCollins.

Mathieu, I. (2011). *Recovering spirituality: Achieving emotional sobriety in your spiritual practice.* Center City, MN: Hazelden.

Milgram, S. (1974). *Obedience to authority.* New York: Harper & Row.

Perls, F. S. (1969). *Gestalt therapy verbatim.* Moab, UT: Real People Press.

Polster, E. (2005). *A population of selves: A therapeutic exploration of personal diversity.* Gouldsboro, ME: Gestalt Journal Press.

Polster, E., & Polster, M. (1973). *Gestalt therapy integrated: Contours of theory and practice.* New York: Brunner/Mazel.

Satir, V. (1972). *Peoplemaking.* Palo Alto, CA: Science and Behavior Books.

Tiebout, H. (1999). *Harry Tiebout: The collected writings.* Center City, MN: Hazelden.

Trimpey, J. (1994). *The final fix: Addictive voice recognition technique.* Silver Lake, WI: Lotus Press.

Volkow, N. D., & Koob, G. (2015). Brain disease model of addiction: Why is it so controversial? *Lancet, 2*(8): 677–679.

Welwood, J. (2002). *Toward a psychology of awakening: Buddhism, psychotherapy, and the path of personal and spiritual transformation.* Boston: Shambhala Publications.

Wilson, B. (1988). The greatest gift of all (pp. 233–236) and The next frontier: Emotional sobriety (pp. 236–238). In *The language of the heart: Bill W.'s* Grapevine *writings* (hardcover ed.). New York: AA Grapevine.

Yontef, G. M. (1993). *Awareness, dialogue & process: Essays on Gestalt therapy.* New York: Gestalt Journal Press.

The Twelve Steps of Alcoholics Anonymous

1. We admitted we were powerless over alcohol—that our lives had become unmanageable.
2. Came to believe that a Power greater than ourselves could restore us to sanity.
3. Made a decision to turn our will and our lives over to the care of God *as we understood Him.*
4. Made a searching and fearless moral inventory of ourselves.
5. Admitted to God, to ourselves, and to another human being the exact nature of our wrongs.
6. Were entirely ready to have God remove all these defects of character.
7. Humbly asked Him to remove our shortcomings.
8. Made a list of all the persons we had harmed, and became willing to make amends to them all.
9. Made direct amends to such people whenever possible, except when to do so would injure them or others.
10. Continued to take personal inventory and when we were wrong promptly admitted it.
11. Sought through prayer and meditation to improve our conscious contract with God *as we understood Him,* praying only for knowledge of His will for us and the power to carry that out.
12. Having had a spiritual awakening as the result of these steps, we tried to carry this message to alcoholics, and to practice these principles in all our affairs.

The Twelve Steps are taken from *Alcoholics Anonymous,* 4th ed. (New York: Alcoholics Anonymous World Services, 2001), 59–60.

About the Author

Allen Berger, Ph.D., is a leading expert in the science of recovery from addiction. Sober since 1971, Berger was part of a pioneering recovery program for Marines returning from Vietnam with alcohol and other drug addictions—first as a participant, then as a counselor. Since then he has become a thought leader in the field, working in clinical settings and private practice. In demand as a speaker, workshop presenter, and interviewee, Berger is well-known in recovery circles among those in recovery as well as therapists and clinicians around the world. He has lectured and written extensively on the process of recovery, emotional sobriety, and the therapeutic value of the Twelve Steps.

About Hazelden Publishing

As part of the Hazelden Betty Ford Foundation, Hazelden Publishing offers both cutting-edge educational resources and inspirational books. Our print and digital works help guide individuals in treatment and recovery, and their loved ones. Professionals who work to prevent and treat addiction also turn to Hazelden Publishing for evidence-based curricula, digital content solutions, and videos for use in schools, treatment programs, correctional programs, and electronic health records systems. We also offer training for implementation of our curricula.

Through published and digital works, Hazelden Publishing extends the reach of healing and hope to individuals, families, and communities affected by addiction and related issues.

For more information about Hazelden publications,
please call **800-328-9000**
or visit us online at **hazelden.org/bookstore**.

Also by This Author

12 Stupid Things That Mess Up Recovery

In simple, down-to-earth language, Allen Berger explores the twelve most commonly confronted beliefs and attitudes that can sabotage recovery. He then provides tools for working through these problems in daily life.
Item 3001
136 pages

12 Smart Things to Do When the Booze and Drugs Are Gone

The author of the recovery mainstay *12 Stupid Things That Mess Up Recovery* offers a fresh list of smart things to do to attain and sustain emotional sobriety.
Item 2864
192 pages